WONDER LEADS

Remarkable lead generation for positive small businesses

DAVE HOLLOWAY

To Jackson & Sophie,
and all the adventures that await

ISBN 978-1-8381175-0-4 (Print edition)

British Library Cataloguing-in-Publication data
A catalogue record for this book is available from the British Library

The purpose of this book is to provide the reader with general information
about the subject matter presented. This book is not intended, nor should the user
consider it, to be legal advice for a specific situation.

The author, company and publisher make no representations or warranties with
respect to the accuracy, fitness, completeness or applicability of the
contents of this book. The author, company and publisher shall in no event be
held liable for any loss or other damages, including but not limited to special, incidental,
consequential, or other damages. Please consider carefully any advice the author
gives before applying it in your workplace.

Cover Design: Dave Holloway
Typeset in Alda OT CEV and Filson Soft by BML Creative, Leeds

First published in 2020 by Jolly Funnel Books
www.jollyfunnel.com

CONTENTS

INTRODUCTION

The typical technician-turned-business-owner: that's the best way to describe my sales technique. I have always been confident talking to prospects about the subjects I know well, and I've been fortunate to win a few relatively sizeable contracts in my time. However, I have never held a pure sales or business development role for any organisation. I am responsible for business development within my company, but it's just one of the many hats I have to wear. Let's just say I was not born to be in sales.

I am not obsessed by targets or closing deals. I hate over-promising. I hate interrupting people. I hate making people feel like a number, and I hate pressurising them. Why? Because *every single time* someone else does those things to me, I *hate* it. And every time it happens – which is a lot when you are running a business – I lose a little more faith in the traditional ways of contacting a cold prospect.

Still, I am a businessman, and being successful in any business requires the ability to attract customers. Which is why I believe that when you have created something of genuine value which can help other businesses to succeed, you are performing a service by bringing it to the attention of the people who can benefit. Continually going above and beyond for customers is the best way to build a business; but sometimes, situations and circumstances dictate proceedings. Sometimes, necessity demands you to be proactive in business development, instead of merely sitting back and waiting for the right people to hunt you down.

How is it possible to accomplish this without resorting to all the things that I – like so many other business professionals – hate about outbound sales?

For more than ten years running my own business, I found myself struggling with this puzzle – and not just any business, a *marketing agency* no less. Not only was I routinely experiencing personal business development headaches, but I had daily exposure to the attempts of clients who were trying to wrestle with their own.

Over the years I tried everything my time and budget would allow: cold calling, email marketing, networking, direct mail, exhibitions, advertising and public relations all played various roles in my ever-evolving business development playbook. All ended up costing me a lot in both time and money, with little reward to show for it. Social media offered me a glimmer of hope, but it's so saturated with ill-conceived, generic sales tactics that it was proving increasingly difficult to cut through the noise.

In truth, the reason this book exists is primarily through desperation. I was desperate for a way to actively generate quality B2B leads for my business. Desperate to fight against the generic, one-size-fits-all spam that plagues my inbox and in-tray daily. Desperate to avoid wasting time and money, neither of which I could afford to lose. Desperate to measure effectiveness, instead of repeatedly flinging mud against a wall in the hope that some of it would stick.

Above all, I was desperate to leave the people I approached with a lasting, positive impression of me and my business – reputations are built over years, yet can be destroyed in minutes. Even the highest echelons of the business world acknowledge they deserve our protection.[1]

In this book I'm going to share with you the framework that finally gave me the breakthrough I had been searching for all those years. A method that enabled me to achieve a reach rate of 55 per cent, a response rate of 44 per cent and a lead-generation rate of nearly 11 per cent. The results proved to be almost 20 times more effective than cold calling.

Best of all, the whole process allowed me to keep my integrity firmly intact.

I hope that Wonder Leads gives you the skills and confidence to go out there and build positive connections with the people that matter to your business.

If the whole world could do that, who knows what incredible things we might all accomplish.

PART
I

BUSINESS DEVELOPMENT BOOT CAMP

5

1

The state of B2B lead generation

Leads are the lifeblood of any B2B business. Without a steady stream of new enquiries, a business can quickly find itself stagnating, unable to manoeuvre with freedom, or overly-dependent on a small customer base. Lead generation is not just the domain of professional sellers and marketeers, it is the business owners ticket to growth, control and security.

What is a B2B lead?

This may seem a pretty daft question to begin a guide on B2B lead generation. If you're interested enough to be reading this, it's probably because you know exactly what a B2B lead is – you just haven't got as many as you want. However, the way you define a B2B lead might not be the same way I would; so, as we are going to be referring to B2B leads a lot during this book, let's just take a moment to check we're both on the same page!

I would summarise a B2B lead as:

> *Direct contact from a potential customer, where there is a genuine opportunity to do business.*

I've split this statement into two halves, which are worth deconstructing:

1. *Direct contact from a potential customer* – meaning someone you could realistically sell your products and services to, proactively communicating with you or your business. It doesn't matter who made the first contact; the important part is that the potential customer must have actively participated in the conversation.

2. *Where there is a genuine opportunity to do business* – meaning the potential customer has expressed real interest in the products and services you provide. That doesn't guarantee business, just the possibility of taking the conversation forward (in sales parlance, a 'warm lead').

Again, this might seem pretty obvious, but my time in networking circles has showed me that people tend to have a pretty loose concept of what constitutes a B2B lead.

For example, it certainly doesn't constitute getting any kind of reply, such as a 'hello' or being kind enough to let you speak: that's just a *conversation*. It certainly doesn't constitute a tip-off from a friend to contact someone they've been talking to down the pub, who happened to mention they might need someone who does what you do: that's simply a *referral*. It certainly doesn't constitute digital metrics such as button clicks and page visits: those are just *engagements*.

All of these things could turn into leads one day, but until the customer actively says something like "This is great, I'd like to find out more", all you have are loose threads to pull on, not leads.

In truth, a B2B lead is straightforward to spot when you see one. The problem is that, much like intelligent political debate or laser discs, genuine B2B leads have been increasingly difficult to come by over the years.

The problem with traditional business development

Business development is a tough profession. It doesn't just require the ability to sell, but a fundamental grasp of the value your company delivers – which isn't always as easy as it sounds.

In B2B businesses, sales often revolve around a complex,

nuanced sales proposition – and it's key not to underestimate our ability to communicate the genuine value of that proposition effectively and succinctly. It's frustrating that business development professionals often rely on prospecting techniques that end up undermining the very value they work so hard to communicate.

To help illustrate this issue, let's take a closer look at some of the methods that currently lead the way in traditional, outbound business development.

THE FEAR OF COLD CALLING

The phone is the most popular tool for outbound sales approaches, but saying it's a rather blunt instrument is a bit like calling the Taj Mahal a lump of stone.

> Evidence from Gordon Tredgold on Entrepreneur.com, who signed up for an experiment to carry out a staggering 2,000 B2B cold calls in just 20 days (just writing that makes me shudder), suggests you need to make an average of 17 calls before successfully speaking to the target.[1] When he finally did manage to get through, Gordon's average appointment setting rate was one in ten. He had to dial 17 times to get through and 90 per cent of the time, the call came to nothing.
>
> In other words, 12 provisional meetings arranged from 2,000 calls.

Seventeen calls. Now, you might have the time, staff, determination and, dare I say, cast-iron nerve to dial this many times just to connect with the right person, but ask yourself:

- Are they going to be happy to listen?
- What will be their state of mind when you do get lucky and start that conversation?
- Are they ready to hear from you?

- Have they stopped working on that urgent project they need to finish today, or finished that report they need to prepare in time for their morning meeting?
- Will it make their life easier to park all of these immediate priorities to engage in a conversation with you?

No, it will not. There is more to think about here than just the paltry number of leads generated. Consider the collateral damage of making 17 calls to the same company before you do finally get to speak to the prospect: 16 times you are likely to talk to a colleague of your target instead; and 15 times the person you talk to will probably moan to everyone in their vicinity about being hounded by Company X *again*.

Is that the type of conversation that you want other people to be having about your business? (It's certainly not one I want anyone to be having about mine!)

I have tried cold calling several times in the past and I'll be frank, all I felt was *fear*. It wasn't nerves, because I know that feeling well: I'm used to presenting in front of people, and I always get a bit nervous beforehand. The fear I experienced when cold calling was something different: the fear of knowing there's an excellent chance that you're about to get on somebody's bad side.

You could say I just needed to get over it, but I don't believe that a body has that kind of visceral reaction unless it's trying to warn you against something horrible. Still, I did it, because that's what all the advice out there tells you to do: 'Just dial, man.'

Well, I did, and I could feel myself shrinking every time someone answered curtly. Life's too short to engage in activities that negatively impact your self-esteem – especially when the chance of reward is so slim.

That's why I am never cold calling anyone again.

THE TRAGEDY OF EMAIL MARKETING

I'm going to cut to the chase here. Email might be the way that business gets done, but it certainly isn't the way to contact cold B2B prospects. It's simply far too saturated with junk.

It doesn't matter if you have the best product in the world, if you try to announce it by bombing people with unsolicited marketing emails, they won't hear you. Probably the only thing that will is their inbox filtering rules.

> Oversaturation is the reason that even the e-marketing gods themselves, Mailchimp, are happy to publish[2] that a click-rate of just 3 per cent is good going for the average email campaign. That includes the ones where the recipients have actively chosen to hear from the sender.

If you are approaching someone cold (which is illegal if they haven't explicitly opted to hear from you, now that the General Data Protection Regulation (GDPR) is in force), then you can be pretty darn sure that the clicks you receive will be far less than that.

The other problem with email is that click rates are the headline metric that everyone uses to indicate success, but a click most certainly *doesn't* indicate a lead. If you are selling B2C, then yes – a click may suggest that the customer has an interest in a particular product that could lead to a sale. But as mentioned previously, if you are selling B2B – especially with a sophisticated service proposition – clicks are simply signals of engagement. That is often a million miles away from a genuine sales opportunity.

A click indicates a vague interest in the content of your message, enough perhaps to warrant a quick nosey round your website; but it's no guarantee that the recipients are interested in buying from you. Maybe they're suffering from fat thumbs and did it by mistake. Perhaps they visited your site and immediately realised your company wasn't the right fit. It could be that they wanted to find your contact details, so they could call you up and make sure you never burden them with your presence again. There's no real way of telling.

> I have indulged in many e-marketing efforts in my time: everything from newsletters to promotional campaigns, mostly targeted at our customer base. Because of my creative background, I've always had high expectations of the results we would get. We took the time to craft compelling, well-designed and thoughtful looking communications, but no matter what we tried, the results were always the same: a handful of clicks to our website, followed by a healthy dose of 'unsubscribe' notifications.
>
> Before the days of GDPR, when it was still legal to approach people by email without their consent, I even tried contacting some cold prospects by email. The results were even more depressing: fewer clicks, yet more 'unsubscribe' notifications and a healthy dose of the dreaded 'spam' marks attached to our account.
>
> I became disillusioned with spending time creating content that nobody ever saw, so when GDPR came into force, I took it as an ideal opportunity to park my email marketing efforts for good.
>
> I've certainly never regretted it.

THE GAMBLE OF DIRECT MAIL

I have a soft spot for direct mail, but that's probably because I'm a designer and love the feel of a great piece of print. I also appreciate all the time and skill that goes into crafting something brilliant with which other people can physically engage.

Unfortunately, most of the time, the direct mail that clogs up my postbox is the very opposite of brilliant. In the vast majority of circumstances, it's dull, unimaginative and generic —so much so, that it goes straight in the recycling, simply because the cover or wrapper tells me all I need to know about the quality of the message that lurks inside. I would be amazed if I'm alone.

It's also worth noting that I run a small business, one where I still open my mail. In many large organisations, mail could be opened by personal assistants and secretaries who might discard it before it even reaches the gaze of the intended recipient. And that has always been my nagging issue with direct mail: it's so incredibly difficult to measure.

> The Data & Marketing Association (DMA) is one of the global authorities in this area. It regularly releases response rate reports indicating the level of performance that marketers can expect from direct mail.
>
> On the face of it, the statistics seem relatively respectable: its 2017 report claims an average response rate from prospect lists of 2.9 per cent.[3] Couple this with numerous other persuasive arguments, including excellent view and retention rates, and there seems to be quite a compelling case for using direct mail.
>
> That is, until you start asking: does the same apply to B2B?

As impressive as these statistics might seem, they are undeniably focused on B2C direct mail. Most comments within the DMA reports relate to households and how their inhabitants respond to marketing post; there is little evidence to indicate that B2B marketers enjoy the same sort of results. During the research for this book, I haven't been able to find a single, specific report giving credible evidence of response rates for B2B direct mail campaigns, let alone any data that indicate expected lead-generation rates.

Here's my other gripe against direct mail: generally, response rate metrics are taken from trackable phone numbers, offer codes and URLs. Indeed, all valid indications of response, *but not all of those responses result in a lead.*

If somebody calls you, there is a pretty good chance they are interested in what you're offering. Similarly, if they take the time to send a postal response, you can probably chalk one up in the lead column. But again, as we identified previously, a tracked URL click is simply a signal of engagement.

And therein lies the problem. While direct mail has the potential to deliver results, in the majority of circumstances it suffers from poor execution, and is almost impossible to measure accurately. For a medium that requires the highest financial investment of all comparative methods, that's a significant mental hurdle to overcome. It's especially true if your financial resources are always on the tighter side.

> The direct mail campaigns that I've used for my own business have never yielded the results I had hoped for: they've been costly to print, mail and in terms of the time invested. I've never known exactly how many have reached the intended recipient, and my loathing of cold calling has made it difficult to follow up.
>
> I'm not ruling out using direct mail again someday, but for now it presents me with serious underlying questions and no suitable answers.

THE EXPENSIVE PULL OF THE TRADE SHOW

Ah, the trade show: the familiar staple of any B2B sales team calendar. Not only does it present an opportunity to display your wares to a niche audience, but it gives you an excellent excuse to escape the office and sample some of the local beverages (purely for research purposes, of course!).

> Undoubtedly, the statistics relating to trade shows are compelling. According to the Event Marketing 2019: Benchmarks and Trends report published by Bizzabo, 84 per cent of leadership – vice-president and C-Suite – believe in-person events to be a critical component of their company's success.[4]

Of trade show attendees, 81 per cent have buying authority,[5] 64 per cent are not customers of the exhibitors' companies;[6] and 72 per cent participate to get leads from new buyers
and prospects.[7] Meanwhile, 77 per cent of executive decision-makers found at least one new supplier at the last show
they attended.[8]

So that's it then, case closed! We just need to book ourselves
into every trade show we can, kick back and watch the leads pour in...
But wait: don't book those flights just yet.* These figures might sound
great, but they aren't immune to scrutiny.

First, buying authority is only relevant if that person is responsible for buying what you sell. They might have a budget for an
entirely different division – which means a conversation might be a
good starting point – but it doesn't necessarily indicate a sales qual-
ified lead.

Second, while 84 per cent of senior executives view trade shows
as central to their company's success, the report doesn't say why this
might be the case. Another statistic from leading exhibitor training organisation, FaceTime, shows that perception of brands that
are absent from events can fall by as much as 5 per cent.[9] Given the
importance of perception in all buying decisions, this could well be
the case; but it also may indicate that the main reason senior executives need a presence at trade shows is to maintain or enhance market
presence. Indeed, this is a strong motive in its own right, but by no
means a sign that trade shows provide an endless supply of quality,
new sales opportunities.

Third, three-quarters of execs may have found a new supplier
at the last show they attended, but the report doesn't say how evenly
the pie is shared out. It could be that a small percentage of exhibitors
snaffled up the vast majority of leads. There is no guarantee that your
business will be among the lucky ones.

Fourth, two-thirds of attendees at the average trade show may
be prospects. Conversely, a good portion could be from competitors
or salespeople from different companies looking to generate leads

---

* At the time of writing, the global Covid-19 pandemic has forced a dramatic shift in the way that
we do business. For the time being, trade shows, large gatherings and face-to-face meetings
have been cancelled, largely replaced by virtual conferences and online, virtual interaction. The
situation remains unclear: if and when normality resumes, readers should follow their respective
government and scientific advice and guidelines as to safe operation.

from exhibitors. If you've done a trade show before, then you will definitely know what I mean.

Finally, 92 per cent of trade show attendees say they are looking primarily for new products,[10] so going to a trade show armed with the next big thing should always be the main objective. However, this presents a significant challenge for many companies which might not be at the forefront of product development.

One thing that escapes all of the above statistics is the cost of exhibiting at a trade show: they usually require significant investment, one way or another. According to a report by Forrester, in-person events take the largest share of B2B marketing budgets at 18 per cent.[11] Typically, the more niche they are, the more expensive they become. You have to shell out for space, the stand, staff, marketing materials, travel, accommodation, not to mention all the time planning before you even get there. More established companies may be able to soak up these costs, but the smaller your team and budget gets, the more the outlay becomes increasingly difficult to justify.

It seems only prudent to ask: can this time and these resources be used more effectively?

Of attendees, 46 per cent frequent only one trade show a year.[12] It's a good sign that trade shows generally attract a more targeted audience, with a higher chance of the right type of person attending – but this places an awful lot of emphasis on a relatively small period of activity. It begs the question: what do you rely on in the periods in-between shows? You can't just assume a bank of high-quality leads to indulge at leisure. You may be lucky to have a few hot ones to pursue, but these often require immediate action. It's highly unlikely that exhibiting once a year will supply the steady stream of leads that all businesses crave.

The other thing that often gets forgotten is that the number of delegates is meaningless if you don't get to speak to them. It doesn't matter if every person who walks in the conference hall is your perfect customer – if they don't take the time to come and talk with you, if they spend all their time in the hospitality tent or watching speakers, all the effort and expense you have gone to counts for nothing.

We exhibited at a business event recently. I can honestly say that we spent months preparing for it. We planned the stand, the literature we needed to create and give away, the competition we would run to capture people's details. We even planned how long we would spend talking to each person, so we didn't miss out on any potential leads. By the time the morning of the event arrived, I genuinely couldn't have been happier with it all.

And you know what, it worked. We came away with details of more than 70 people, and followed up with every one – the only problem was, nobody was interested in what we did. For the most part they were present for their own purposes: spreading news of their businesses and scouting out competitors. It cost me several months of planning, production of a new stand, loads of printed material and a whole day at the show with three team members, and we didn't generate one single sales opportunity from it.

I'm not saying that my experience is typical of everyone exhibiting at trade shows; perhaps it's more indicative of the event we chose. Nonetheless, that experience – together with all the other information I know about trade show marketing – means I am unlikely to be dusting off our exhibition stand anytime soon.

THE NETWORKING TIME DRAIN

Either you love networking, or you hate it. Whichever camp you reside in, on the face of it at least, it's easy to see why people love it.

According to global face-to-face networking organisation, BNI, its 255,000 members worldwide traded more than 11 million referrals in 2019, generating $15.7 billion in business.[13] And that makes perfect sense, because according to Forbes Insights, 84 per cent of people prefer face-to-face business meetings to technology-enabled ones.[14]

> When asked why, the same survey found that 85 per cent of respondents felt that face-to-face meetings presented the opportunity to build stronger, more meaningful business relationships.

And that is where the power of networking really lies. Being face-to-face with someone allows you to benefit from the full gamut of communication tools at your disposal. Not only do you have the chance to listen to what people say, but understand how it is being delivered. If the person is leaning towards you with their head tilted slightly forward, and they are holding regular eye contact, the chances are you have their attention. If they are leaning away from you, have their arms crossed and constantly gaze around the room while you are talking to them, there's a good chance they've zoned out.

The same applies in reverse. You have the opportunity to make a far greater impression on the people you speak with face-to-face than you would do if using words alone.

> *The problem is, it doesn't matter how brilliant an impression you make if you aren't speaking to the right people at the right time.*

Which is precisely why business development through networking is a much bigger challenge than the statistics might suggest.

There is certainly no shortage of networking groups in the average business community. From private associations and trade bodies to government-led initiatives, ample opportunities exist to interact with any number of professionals in a wide variety of formal and informal situations. These are brilliant if your business is happy to sell anything to anyone, regardless of budget or quality of work required. If you have a more complex service proposition, expertise in specific markets and need to talk to people in specific roles, wish to limit your geographic focus and the time when you meet, or hope to sell on value rather than price – you're likely to find appropriate networking opportunities much harder to come by.

It's widely recognised that networking is a highly unpredictable method of generating leads. When someone else is in charge of the schedule, we can't guarantee that attendees will be right for our business – and even if they are, whether we'll even get a chance to converse with them.[15] And that really sums up the problem with networking as a business development tool. It *can* work, but it's extremely difficult to say *when*. As a result, the only option to those who are serious about networking is to persevere with attending week in, week out. Depending on the circumstances and events being targeted, this often requires a huge time investment.

> *If you aren't comfortable spending a high percentage of time speaking to the wrong people, networking is not the option for you.*

I have always struggled to find the right networking groups. It's a piece of cake finding a networking group for fellow creatives, but if I want to attend one with, say, managing directors of manufacturing companies with a £10 million-plus turnover, based within a 30-mile radius of my own location, the opportunities become infinitely smaller (or should I say, non-existent).

As a result, I've always had to settle for broader groups. Invariably, they lack a high enough concentration of the right type of people to justify the considerable time I needed to invest in attending.

Time is the one resource I lack the most: as I've mentioned, networking requires a tremendous amount, usually outside of regular business hours when I want to be with my family. For me at least, the output has never justified sacrificing the excessive time to be there.

THE HIGH COST OF ADVERTISING

Advertising is one of the oldest forms of business development. Ancient Egyptians used papyrus to make sales messages and wall posters. Archaeologists have uncovered commercial notices from the ruins of Pompeii and relics of adverts from ancient Greece. It's no surprise that advertising dominated business development for much of the 20th century.

Back when the *Yellow Pages* was the only way to find a business, the best development tactic was to start a company called 'AA Anything'. The next best was taking out the biggest advert possible, preferably on the front or back cover. Get these two things right and it was only a matter of time before the leads would start to follow.

Oh, if only things were still that simple. Times have changed since the golden days of advertising, but for many people it remains the preferred method of reaching customers. The only difference is the form it takes.

A 2019 report by Zenith Media predicted global advertising spend to reach $623 billion by the end of 2019.[16] Of that figure, traditional advertising, including TV, radio, newspapers, magazines, billboards and other outdoor media still accounted for the majority of that spend. However, this is unlikely to be the case for much longer. In many countries including the UK, China and the USA, digital has already become the dominant advertising medium.

By 2021, Zenith predicts that internet advertising will account for 49 per cent of global advertising spend. It would certainly be no great shock to see it top the charts by 2022.[17]

These are tremendous numbers. There is no doubt that advertising remains a viable option for an awful lot of businesses, but the real question is: is it viable for B2B – especially for the smallest businesses?

The first thing to note is that according to eMarketer, B2B digital advertising spending only accounts for 4.6 per cent of the global digital advertising market.[18] Advertising is a consumer-dominated medium – and that makes sense, as the average B2C consumer group is pretty substantial. When eyes on product is the number one consideration, advertising is the only option. The problem is, for the majority of B2B companies, the target audience groups are much smaller because targets lie *within* targets.

If all the people working at a company were viable targets, audience groups would be pretty sizeable. Sadly, anyone who works in B2B business development knows this isn't the case. There are usually only one or two primary decision-makers for any particular purchase, often assisted by a few other colleagues of influence. Which means for every company – even the ones employing thousands of people – only a small handful of individuals actually matter. That's when advertising becomes a more challenging proposition.

Print media is particularly susceptible here, because tracking return on investment (ROI) is so difficult. How can you know if the full-page advert you have spent thousands on ever passed the gaze of Joe Bloggs, Human Resources Manager at ABC Corp? The reality is, you can't. In the majority of circumstances, all you can do is hope. The statistics would indicate that more and more B2B businesses are wising up to the difficulty of proving that ROI.

> According to the Business Information Network (BIN) report released by Connectiv, the annual revenue generated by B2B print advertising in the USA fell by more than half, from just under $10 billion in 2008 to $4.9 billion in 2017.[19] The trend is a continuing decline.
>
> In the same period, digital advertising has gone the other way entirely, from less than $2 billion in 2008 to $6.8 billion in 2017. The reason is the continued digitisation of our economy, together with the improved targeting options now available.

It's certainly easier to track ROI on digital, because you have access to click metrics. As we've already seen, clicks correspond to visits, which turn into enquiries and finally end up as leads. Or do they? They could be clicks from job hunters, competitors, suppliers or even your own staff. They could be one of the 34 per cent of consumers that HubSpot claims have mistakenly clicked on an ad.[20]

The truth is, none of these people care whether it costs you $2 or $20 for them to visit your website. The advertising company certainly doesn't. This is precisely the type of event which can end up making digital advertising so incredibly expensive. You aren't just paying for clicks; you're fighting for those clicks against every other business on the planet – and if they have deeper pockets than you, the only way you can compete is to add a few inches to your own. Unless you operate in an ideological market of high margins, high volume and a high number of customers, it can be a road to misery.

> According to the leading online advertising platform, WordStream, the most expensive keywords in Google Advertising and Bing Ads cost $50 or more per click.[21] These are usually highly competitive keywords in industries with high customer lifetime values, such as law and insurance.

While some insurance and law firms have the margins to absorb such high customer acquisition costs, there is absolutely no way that every business does. Paying $50 for a single click is the perfect example of what happens when several exceptionally well-funded bidders compete for the same prize. Market forces simply push up the price to whoever wants to pay the most, and the only real winner is the media company. The ones who suffer the most are the smaller players on the fringes who can least afford to lose.

> My business makes up part of the two-thirds of people whom marketing insight experts, The Manifest, states have invested in online advertising.[22] I've dabbled in Facebook, Twitter, Instagram and LinkedIn. But by far and away the most time and money I've invested has gone into Google Ads.

I have shown so much faith in Google Adwords that at one point, I was spending nearly £1000 a month to try and generate enquiries through my website. This might not sound like a lot to many people, especially when WordStream say in the same article that the average small business spends between $9,000 and $10,000 a month on advertising. Nonetheless, to me it was a significant investment – enough to warrant getting some one-on-one attention from Google's own Adwords success team.

I followed every piece of advice they gave me. I set an appropriate budget, made sure my ads were fitting and accurately targeted, using comprehensive keywords. I improved my quality scores, added extensions, disabled poor-performing ads, and monitored all of this daily.

While I saw clicks going through, they seldom turned into leads. I'm convinced that most of the clicks I got were from competitors or job hunters, because I always saw spikes in speculative job applications while running campaigns, despite excluding every variant of 'job vacancy' known to humankind from my account.

Ultimately, this campaign failed to deliver what it promised. It proved to me that I could not expect to turn on the 'lead tap' through Google Ads – at least not without spending the kind of money which could have taken years to see a return.

This is the final thing I have to say about advertising:

> *You can throw all the money you want at it, but it's still a highly reactive medium.*

All you can do is pay your money and keep your fingers crossed that the right people will engage with you. If they don't, it's just money down the drain.

THE CURSE OF SOCIAL MEDIA

Before you start shouting at the page (or screen, if you're using an e-reader), I know: social media is a marketing task, not one for sales. Technically, you're correct – but the truth is, the lines between sales and marketing are so blurred that in most instances, it's difficult to separate one from the other.

After all, cold calls require scripts and follow-up materials, which usually involve marketing input. A sales leaflet drop requires something tangible to put in the post. E-marketing requires someone to create an email. Trade shows need someone to build the stand. Even networking requires someone to provide business cards to hand out. Whether you do these things yourself, use an agency or have an internal or external marketing department to do them, you are still engaged in marketing.

Of course, the role of marketing is to create and consistently communicate the company value proposition. And as we've already seen, without a value proposition, sales teams are up the creek. Sales and marketing are inseparable, so social media still makes my list of business development approaches. There a more than a few good reasons why.

> Digital channels now influence 92 per cent of B2B buying decisions.[23] Companies with consistent social selling processes are 40 per cent more likely to hit revenue goals than non-social sellers.[24] Of C-level executives, 84 per cent use social media to make purchasing choices.[25]

These are compelling statistics, especially compared with the alternative options. The Internet and rise of social media have caused the balance of power in sales conversations to shift overwhelmingly to the buyer. In the majority of instances, the 'buying process' as we should probably call it, starts with simply firing up a search engine or social media search page.

> *A good network, strong presence, intelligent thought leadership and active participation in discussion are crucial to improving sales in the modern age.*

Still, while this requires effort in both strategy and execution (after all, you won't have a social media presence if you don't take the time to generate content), it can't be called *proactive* from a sales or business development perspective, because those methods still require someone to stumble across your content. It's a bit like doing a mass door drop: either the intended recipient sees it, or they don't – and it's when you try and force things with social media that the wheels can start to come off.

The whole principle of social media is to build genuine, valuable connections between people located anywhere in the world; but like email, social media is saturated with spammers. I cannot tell you how many generic "Let's connect!" requests, or "Do I have the perfect job for you!" InMails I get from LinkedIn daily (we'll be looking at the pitfalls of InMail in Chapter 6). Worse still, the vast majority of approaches I receive are mass mailouts from people who have never looked at my profile. How can I know that? Because the usual approach is from a recruiter telling me how short they are of great architects in Dubai. Had they actually spent two seconds on my profile, they would have realised my job title at BML (the agency I run with my wife) is 'Brand Architect'. (I like to try my hand at many things, but I'm pretty confident that the citizens of Dubai would be rightly terrified if someone compelled them to live in a house designed by yours truly!)

Unfortunately, this is symptomatic of many people's experience with social media. While it offers an incredible opportunity to build relationships across industries and continents, it is far too easy to abuse. It's those few looking for quick wins which ultimately diminishes the power of social media for everyone.

Maximising social media's undeniable potential requires getting to the heart of why it exists in the first place: the ability to engage other people in *meaningful* conversations. Luckily, we'll be looking at this more closely in Part II.

HELLO
WONDER
LEADS

27

2

How it all got started

Wonder Leads began life as a series of business development experiments motivated by a desire to attract more clients to the strategic branding service offered through our agency work.

Strategic branding is a complex B2B sales proposition. It has the power to transform an organisation's fortunes, but articulating *why* it matters – especially to people without in-depth knowledge of marketing or brand strategy – can be a challenge. It requires significant financial investment, together with the time and attention of the most senior people within a business. Usually the people with the least time to spare, who often see marketing as an expendable cost in their profit and loss statement.

In other words, a tough sell.

I've never had a problem with explaining the value of strategic branding when speaking directly to a prospect. My problem has always been creating opportunities to talk to the right type of prospects in the first place – and I'm not alone. According to research by BrightTALK, increasing the quality and quantity of leads are the main priorities for B2B professionals.[1] But where are they? More to the point, how do you go out and get more of them?

As we've already discussed, numerous ways exist to approach business development; the problem is, none of them work the way that most people want them to work. A 2018 study by HubSpot reports that only 18 per cent of marketers say outbound practices provide the highest quality leads for sales.[2] In other words, traditional, proactive business development might be generating leads, but the vast majority aren't good enough to pursue.

That sums up the situation I found myself. I wanted quality leads, but couldn't afford to waste 80 per cent of my efforts on ineffective approaches.

Then thanks to a couple of random events, everything changed.

A series of fortunate events

The first coincidence happened during a professional visit. I was meeting a chap called Jonathon, who ran a high-growth technology company in Leeds. (For those of you reading outside of the UK, Leeds is a city in the north of England where I work, known for being one of the sunniest places in the northern hemisphere. Ahem.)

We were having a pleasant time, discussing the seemingly limitless cons to running a business, when Jonathon said: "Wait a minute, you should see this." He left the room for a minute, then returned with a package he had been sent in the post earlier that week: a video brochure. If you haven't seen one before, a video brochure is basically a tablet computer surrounded by printed cardboard which plays a video when you open it up. The content on this one was something special.

When he opened up the brochure, a video started playing. It was the CEO of another company speaking to Jonathan. I mean, *really* speaking to Jonathon. His opening line was: "Hello Jonathon." After which he began talking to Jonathon about his company and how it might be able to help him. The video also looked great – filmed in a modern office boardroom with a professional yet relaxed feel. The production was impressive, but it was the level of personalisation which set my mind on fire. They hadn't just recorded one film and sent it out to a massive mailing list. They had taken all the extra time to film, edit, upload and send a personalised copy just for Jonathon – niche marketing at its finest.

Most importantly, Jonathon thought it was great. Impressive enough to keep and show to other people. If that had got the attention of one CEO, could it impress others too? I left the meeting buzzing with ideas, determined to give it a go. As usual, life and other business priorities took over, so the concept remained just that, until about six months later when a second encounter with personalised video revived the idea from its conceptual stasis.

Recently, I had finished reading *Clockwork: Design Your Business to Run Itself* by the bestselling author, Mike Michalowicz:[†] a brilliant, practical guide for business owners looking to improve their operations.[3] I was keen to try and action some of the learning from the book, so signed up to get access.

About three days later, an email appeared from Mike's address: it looked like your typical automated e-marketing funnel, mentioning something about a video. Work was busy, so I ignored it. Then about a week later, another email arrived:

> "Did you get a chance to watch the video? It wasn't a cheesy, generic gimmick. I recorded it just for you."

This sparked my curiosity, so I clicked. The link led to a web page with a video from Mike Michalowicz himself: he greeted me personally, using my name and company. He had recorded the video just for me. It had precisely the same effect as the video brochure that Jonathon had received all those months previously. The whole video was less than 40 seconds long, but it was the most memorable business communication I had ever received.

Early production

Immediately after seeing Mike's video, I knew the idea for a video brochure needed reviving, so decided to invest in a trial. We found a supplier and sent over a design for the print elements. A sample arrived within six weeks, complete with BML branding and a matching protective case. It looked great, but the real work lay ahead – what were we going to put on the video?

As a cold introduction, the content needed to be short and sharp. It had to be a single voice, because the two examples had

---

shown how effective this was at getting a recipient's attention. I was responsible for our business development, so I had to record the message. It was clear that quality and content of delivery would be critical, so we spent a lot of time crafting, experimenting and rehearsing different scripts until finally, one of them felt right. It struck a nice balance between friendly and professional – and most importantly, it felt real.

Next, we turned our attention to filming. The video Jonathon had received was polished, set in a well-chosen scene and shot with professional equipment. The video Mike had sent me looked like it had been filmed on his mobile phone before tucking into his breakfast (clearly, polish was not part of his plan!). Both videos were impressive, but one required more time to execute than the other. Echoing Mike's approach seemed the obvious choice, but on deeper reflection, the impressive thing about his video was *who* he was, not the medium itself. Mike is pretty famous and no doubt very busy, yet he still took the time to record a personalised message for some unknown person on the other side of the Atlantic – which added significantly more value to it.

Would Jonathon have been as impressed with his brochure if the company had filmed his video in the same casual way Mike's had been? No. Our targets would be business leaders who didn't know about us. To make sure we set the perception of value in our service at the right level, we had to make a great first impression: our videos would need to look as good as we could make them.

The only problem was, we had little knowledge of video production. It was a case of learning on the fly. Luckily, we had a digital SLR (DSLR) camera in the studio: it was a few years old, but it shot excellent high-definition (HD) video. Experiments followed, exploring the effect of different locations, viewpoints, lenses, lighting and audio set-ups. Eventually it began to take shape, and before long, we had a pilot introduction, filmed, edited and waiting to go. I uploaded it to the sample brochure and proudly showed the finished product to the team. It was a massive relief. At last it felt like all our business development headaches were coming to an end.

That was until I had a last-minute panic.

Changing lanes

We had put weeks of effort into creating that first video brochure. Now it was ready, I suddenly fell prey to nagging doubts. Video brochures are not cheap. It seemed logical they would get attention, but would they end up in the hands of the right person? Posting them out was always going to be an expensive roll of the dice. The question was: could we afford to lose? Speculation precedes accumulation, but it didn't change the reality of the situation: the prospect of spending several thousand on a completely untested business development approach.

Yes, I'd seen evidence that something similar *could* work in generating a positive response, but was it all just an expensive gimmick? Would anyone else see value in it? Could it create genuine sales opportunities? It seemed increasingly important to test the concept before doubling down on the brochure route.

So, we began exploring ways to deliver the videos *digitally*.

Sailing the digital channels

Our video introduction was a digital file, which begged the question: why was a physical brochure so important? Mike had used an email to get me to visit a web page to view his video. And it had impressed me, despite its rather rough-around-the-edges execution. But as we've already identified, using email as a delivery method is fraught with problems: not least, spam.

It's not the spam as such; rather, the consequences of it that causes issues. Everyone is so desperate to avoid unsolicited rubbish: firewalls restrict unidentified traffic, images are routinely blocked; inbox rules are merciless, and the 'Delete' button is wielded with ruthless efficiency.

That's precisely what I did with the email that first introduced Mike's video: one I liked from someone I knew! I already realised that producing these videos was always going to require time, and that their success or failure would depend on the percentage of people who watched it, not the number created. The open rates and click rates for email marketing were far too low to justify the investment.

We needed something more targeted, focused and with the right concentration of professionals in our target industries. So naturally, I opened up LinkedIn.

The missing link

LinkedIn is the number one social media platform for business professionals around the world, and with good reason.

LinkedIn has 303 million active users per month, 120 million of whom use the platform every day; 61 million users are senior-level influencers, and 40 million are decision-makers. It's the most commonly used social media platform among Fortune 500 companies.[4] It's also a hotbed of B2B activity.

Of B2B marketers, 95 per cent use LinkedIn as a content distribution channel,[5] 59 per cent say that LinkedIn generates leads,[6] while 65 per cent of B2B companies have acquired a customer through LinkedIn.[7] LinkedIn generates more than ten times the number of B2B leads than Facebook.[8]

In short, of all the online platforms in the world, LinkedIn is the place where B2B business gets done. I was already an active LinkedIn user, but my past efforts at using it for proactive business development had always been unsuccessful. Few of the people we reached out to ever responded, and we never generated any work from them. For the past few years, we had purely used LinkedIn for content-sharing, not individual targeting. It felt like this was our best route to success, but it was a slow burner. It was almost impossible to push without spending money on advertising.

Fast forward a few years, and we now had something very different to send to individual prospects. Something that didn't require advertising, but had a high chance of getting their attention. All we had to do was get them to watch.

3

The First Wonder Leads

Land ahoy

Our video introduction script had been built around one of our most robust client case studies. The original plan was to use the video brochure to drive recipients to the case study on our website: once there, they could read about the project in more detail and see both the quality of our work and what we could do.

Of course, I hadn't ruled out the possibility that my video could lead to an immediate business opportunity, but it seemed unrealistic – everyday purchases our business offers not. Companies rebrand every few years, not every few weeks, and the chances of a prospect responding with an immediate, pressing need were remote. The most realistic goal was to plant a small seed which, over time, might turn into an opportunity – but only if the stars aligned for that business.

Initially, we had intended to mail the brochure to the prospect, so they could hold the video (and case study link) in their hands, but that was no longer an option. Instead, we needed to create a digital home for the video: in other words, a landing page. There are countless video hosting platforms out there, and we invested a lot of time in trying out alternatives. Sadly, none of them offered the level of control we needed, either lacking the right degree of customisation and reporting functionality, or burdened with too many distractions.

We needed a bespoke solution, so we decided to use our existing agency website. We built new functionality to create unique, private landing pages for individual videos, and pored over every element of the design. After extensive testing, we'd achieved it: a clear, branded, functional landing page to match the quality of the video it was created to showcase.

All that remained was to see if it worked.

Pressing the button

We focused our efforts on fresh connections, because these approaches could be framed as real introductions. A target profile was drawn up and some carefully worded connection requests dispatched. Within a few days, I had enough new connections to move on to recording.

I blocked out a day to do my first batch of recordings. Once they were filmed and edited, we created our first, real landing pages on our website. They looked strong. It was finally time to send an introduction to a genuine prospect. I opened LinkedIn, composed a personal message to my new connection and inserted the link to their landing page. Then I hovered my mouse over the send button – and kept it there. For what felt like hours.

It was probably less than 2 minutes, but I am sure that my mind played through every conceivable, adverse event that was about to follow that button click. The thing is, you can always find a million reasons to avoid doing something that scares you. But then, a little bit of fear is usually a good indication that you're about to do something that matters.

It took less than 2 hours to realise that little click was going to change *everything*.

Bingo!

The first response arrived within an hour of sending out the first five pilot introductions, from a board-level executive in my target sector. He had read the message, clicked the link, viewed the landing page and watched the video. Even though there wasn't an opportunity for us to work together, he had still taken the time to send a polite reply. It was the sweetest sounding "No" I could ever wish to hear.

About an hour later, it became clear just how successful this new approach could be. Another reply – this time, including a copy of a post that my prospect had added to his public profile. The post showed the link to my video, accompanied by a message he had shared with his *entire* network:

> "Now, this is what I call a professional introduction! David Holloway from BML Creative made this nice surprise video to introduce his company after we connected here on LinkedIn yesterday. Great job, David!"

A quick glance at our website analytics showed the landing page had received dozens of views within a few minutes, while his post had received numerous likes and positive comments, including one from his company's managing director. Once my heart had stopped racing, it became obvious that this was a slice of rare fortune. Instead of just having responses from those five pilot recipients, we now had the validation of many more people – and they unanimously approved.

This told me it worked. That all the thought, effort and attention to detail was going to be worth it.

A friendly nudge

Following this earlier success, we sent out more introductions. It was easy to see from the website analytics that not everyone had visited their landing page, and this posed a problem. How could we encourage people to view their videos without feeling harassed?

We knew the introductions delivered genuine value. They explained how we could help prospects as a business; but the main advantage was that they helped to build a more meaningful relationship. They deserved to be given a second chance. The videos had an inherently positive tone, so any follow-up message needed to be the same: short, polite and upbeat. Instead of thinking of them as follow-ups, we framed them as gentle 'nudges'. If a response was still not forthcoming following a nudge, we would do the right thing – move on to another prospect and leave them in peace. It had integrity.

Within a few hours of sending out my first round of nudges, more replies started to come in: vindication of a gentler approach. In fact, it was more than vindicated. One of them was from the managing director of a large manufacturing business:

> "Dave, I absolutely love this. If I could find the applause emoji, I'd send it. Now isn't the right time, but can you give me a call in March?"

He had even included his mobile number.

I had my first rock-solid lead.

On the record

During the initial stages, we hadn't given much thought to recording our activity. Landing page visits could be easily tracked, and responses appeared directly from LinkedIn's messaging system to my inbox – and that seemed sufficient. But it also seemed obvious that the more videos we created, the more management the process would require. It needed better structure.

Although it was early days, optimisation was starting to enter the frame. Could we learn anything from the videos that got responses to help us generate them more frequently?

For example:

- Did personalisation matter?
- Did it matter when messages were sent out?
- Did clothing choice make a difference?
- What about the choice of filming location?

– all of these questions warranted answers.

We put together a spreadsheet to record this activity. It started off basic, but within a few weeks it had grown far more comprehensive, capturing every kind of data. Staying on top of it took time but the process was worth it, as we needed something to help keep it on track and make it even better.

Now we had a tool that could do just that, at least until something better came along.

Hold that thought

Looking at the data, it became clear that those first, positive responses had not been a fluke. The results coming back were unprecedented:

- Reach rates above 50 per cent
- Overall response rates above 40 per cent
- Response rates from confirmed views at nearly 80 per cent

Most incredibly, warm leads were starting to flow. Total lead generation was hovering at just over 10 per cent – almost 20 times more than you might expect from a cold calling campaign (probably the closest comparable form of proactive business development).[1]

Strangely enough, despite such remarkable results, it still felt like something was missing. The video was a great start, but it didn't leave recipients with anything tangible; all the contact had been at a relatively superficial level.

Could we maximise the impact of those early conversations by providing something more meaningful? The answer was yes: by education.

Adopting an educator role provides two significant benefits. First, it demonstrates expertise, which in turn establishes credibility. Second (and most importantly), it helps a prospect to reach an 'aha!' moment, which is fundamental to building a strong value proposition.

> *If people can't understand what you do and why it matters to them, they simply won't buy. Or rather, they could buy, but inevitably they'll fixate on price.*

Face-to-face conversation with a prospect has always been essential to cementing the value of our business, but that wasn't an option within this new process. We needed another way to demonstrate that value and follow up on the introduction video. So we decided to bookend the process with one final, high-value contact: a quality *insight piece*.

Fortunately, the perfect solution was waiting in the wings: a guide I had written recently, 'Engineering customers',[2] which explained how businesses could influence the inbound B2B sales process to attract more high-value customers. The importance of a company's brand was at the heart of the narrative.

As with the nudges, we needed to keep prospects on-side; so, after a good amount of time, we sent out insight pieces to every-one who had been previously contacted. It was hard to know how many read it, but messages of thanks and positive comments came back from several recipients – even from some who hadn't replied previously.

The process had its ending, it felt complete – but that was just the start.

I had already begun to micro-analyse the process, and was starting to imagine the tools that could be built to make it faster, simpler and even more effective. They may not have had a name, but Wonder Leads was under construction, as was our Socialaser soft-ware. It wasn't yet apparent where this would all go, but it had the potential to leave an indelible, positive mark on the world.

And that's precisely what I set out to achieve.

4

The Wonder Leads Framework

Wonder Leads is a lead-generation framework for small businesses which value people as much as results. It has been designed to help you start generating quality B2B leads in the shortest time possible, regardless of your knowledge or level of experience.

Wonder Leads comprises six core pillars:

1. Connecting
2. Storytelling
3. Filming
4. Publishing
5. Messaging
6. Measuring.

Each one is covered in detail throughout the following chapters. By the end of the book, you will have the knowledge and resources to start implementing Wonder Leads in your business.

I'm sharing this methodology with you now in the hope that, if nothing else, a few of us can make an improvement to the quality of communication out there in the world. At a time when it seems acceptable to say anything you want to anyone you want without fear of the damage it may cause, it seems we could all benefit from a bit more of that.

Before you read any further, some caveats. First, your results might be different to mine, so don't take the figures quoted as gospel – expect some variation. Second, digital tools and technology change pretty fast: while every effort has been made to keep all the information here up-to-date at the time of publishing, inevitably processes change as systems are updated and technology evolves. Be prepared to adapt what is here to your current situation.

The general, underlying principle of Wonder Leads is timeless:

> *To start incredible conversations, ensure every action you take delivers the maximum positive value to the prospect.*

If you do that, Wonder Leads will almost certainly change the way you think about business development forever.

Throughout the following chapters you will find a comprehensive series of worksheets designed to walk you through key aspects of the process. (These are also available in a free pack available for download from the Wonder Leads website: see the Resources section at the end of this book.)

Finally, I've already discussed the merits of LinkedIn as a platform for targeting B2B leads in Chapter 2. Still, you are probably (and rightly) wondering whether I'm affiliated in some way with the platform, and only writing this to boost its user numbers and exposure? I can categorically state that I have no financial or contractual connection to LinkedIn in any way whatsoever. I'm simply a platform user, because it works for me.

OK, now all of that's out of the way, let's get down to the business of generating leads!

PART III

CONNECTING

5

Your LinkedIn Profile

You can't generate leads through LinkedIn without connecting to someone first – and building a network on LinkedIn is a vast topic, enough to write a book about in itself. There are hundreds already out there and a positively medieval feast of blog articles, downloads and forums that explore the topic in every conceivable way. For the sake of brevity (and your sanity), we're just going to concentrate on the most critical steps that will maximise your chances of connecting with the right prospects for your business.

If you are a profile geek and want more information than the following pages provide, just fire up your search engine of choice and type 'how to connect with people on LinkedIn' – you'll almost certainly have enough material to keep you going for the next thousand years.

For everyone else, let's get cracking with the first step in building your network of LinkedIn prospects: the right kind of profile.

Building a positive profile

Before doing anything, it's important for your LinkedIn profile to look the part. People should be drawn to you, not turned away, and profiles should be a positive reflection of the individual and the business they represent. Try examining your profile from the perspective of a potential customer, and asking yourself: "If I were my prospect, would I connect with someone presenting themselves like this?"

A lot of LinkedIn profiles are overly professional, often driven by the fear of looking weak and attracting scornful looks for demonstrating the slightest bit of personality. While I can understand this, the result is that the vast majority of profiles on LinkedIn look and sound the same: really quite dull. I'm not saying for one minute that it's a sensible idea to adorn a horse costume for your profile photo, or substitute your employment history with some witty prose extolling the virtues of your weekly line-dancing classes. However, it's perfectly OK to inject a bit of your natural personality into the virtual face you present to the professional world. I would actively encourage it.

With that in mind, here are some major things to consider when refining your LinkedIn profile.

1. YOUR PROFILE PHOTO

Look happy

For the love of all things, *smile*. It's impossible to underestimate the importance of looking happy in your profile photo. Scientists have found that seeing a smiling face activates the orbitofrontal cortex – the region of the brain that processes sensory rewards – suggesting that when we see another person smiling, our body feels rewarded.[1] Swedish scientists have also found that smiling is contagious, and that it takes a genuine, conscious effort not to return a smile when we see one.[2] That's pretty powerful stuff.

Use good lighting

The technical aspect that makes or breaks any photo is good lighting (discussed further in Chapter 10, 'Location'). Natural light is the best option, as it gives a much warmer feel to your photos – this might mean heading outside. If that isn't an option, then shooting near a window or in a well-lit room will work just fine.

Don't be shy

I appreciate that even in the narcissistic world of reality TV and self-ies we now seem to inhabit that there are vast numbers of people who recoil as soon as they're put in front of a camera. Try to set any negative thoughts you might have to one side: after all, it's only a box with a bit of glass attached! If possible, enlist a partner, colleague, family member or close friend to take a load of shots with the best camera you can get hold of, and keep going until one of them looks natural. It might take an hour or two of feeling a little exposed, but it will be worth it.

2. YOUR HEADER IMAGE

Right at the top of your profile, LinkedIn has placed a handy, although rather fiendishly sized, header image. Finding the right image to drop into this space can be tricky, due to the extreme panoramic format: this is why many people just opt for one of the default colours or texture images. While the size inevitably limits the options, I would advise making use of this, as it helps bring a profile to life visually.

Make it different

Good header images should contrast with the profile image. A shot of you at work, delivering training, at a speaking engagement or engaging with your team can all make compelling header images. It could even be a more inspirational shot of you outside of work. Whatever you choose, make sure it is another quality image and that it fits well as a panorama. There is no point opting for that fantastic portrait on the summit of Everest if all anyone can see is a leg and some snow! It's better to pick a slightly less dynamic image that fits the space well. Wider shots, as opposed to close-ups, are your friends here.

3. YOUR HEADLINE

Nothing sparks as much debate as a LinkedIn headline: the title appearing next to your profile image whenever you show up in another user's feed. Crucially, this is what people see next to your name and profile photo when you try to connect with them. Because this will be one of the first things that people see about you, it has significance.

There are different schools of thought here, and as ever, the advice is to go with whatever feels most natural.

_____

Highlight the problems you solve

The first option is to highlight the problems your business helps to solve. Let's imagine you are a small digital marketing agency working with start-ups. Your headline might read something like:

> "Helping start-ups to drive growth through effective digital content"
> Or:
> "Giving start-ups the creative tools to communicate online"

Having a brand with a clearly defined value proposition can help enormously here, because brand positioning statements can be repurposed to fit your requirements.

_____

Use your current job title

The other (and far less time-consuming) approach is to use your current job title. It's the most common method, for the simple reason that LinkedIn uses the current job title by default. If you prefer the simple route, it might be a good idea to tweak your default headline a little so that it rolls off the tongue more easily.

> I use the former method because it's less common, more personal and helps me to stand out better. It also helps to avoid people reading too much into my job title.

> Titles such as 'director' sound official and vague, which personally is the last thing I want people to think about me.
>
> If your job title is 'sales manager' or some other name that often acts as a klaxon for a mass-prospect departure, this approach might help you to remove a little bit of that unwanted stigma.

4. YOUR BIO

Nothing keeps the good citizens of LinkedIn more awake at night than wondering what to put in their bio. Your bio provides an excellent opportunity to reinforce the positive experience that people might have when they interact with you.

Like a good headline, a good bio explains the problems that a person helps people to overcome, and the types of things that drive them. This approach helps others to understand you a lot more than listing every award nomination, or an in-depth description of daily duties at work.

Everyone is busy. Your bio is simply there to reinforce the positive reasons for people to connect.

5. PROFILE HOUSEKEEPING

While the above are the main components to worry about, a few general other points are worth considering to help keep your profile looking tip-top.

Keep your résumé current

There is nothing wrong with a touch of romantic retrospection, but if your headline and bio still reference a job role from six years ago, new connections are going to be confused. Do keep it current, so prospects get a real impression of what you are up to now.

Nothing gets people scratching their heads more than significant gaps in a résumé. Of course, this doesn't mean including that Saturday job at Woolworths 26 years ago, but it is an excellent idea just to make sure your career and education history is complete.

Ask clients for recommendations

While it's great and often necessary to blow your own trumpet, it's more powerful if other people do the trumpet-blowing for us. 'Recommendations', as LinkedIn calls them, can be great additions to a profile, as they give third-party validation to both professional skills and character. I am not convinced that Recommendations greatly influence an individual's decision to connect or not; but still, a ringing endorsement from a client or colleague can't do any harm.

Create and share great content

We make connections when we think that people will add value to our network. On LinkedIn, your content-sharing activity appears high up on your profile, so inevitably it's one of the first things that people will see. It increases your chances of connecting if that content is relevant to the people with whom you want to connect, so try to make sure there is a high percentage of industry-specific activity in your feed. That way, when your prospect looks at your profile and sees what you are up to, they'll be more inclined to think: "This person seems like they know my world pretty well." They'll believe that you share similarities: people generally build their networks with others who are likeminded. You can back this up further by creating articles which also have prominence at the top of your feed.

> *Insightful, industry-specific articles are great for reinforcing your industry specialism and enhancing perceived expertise.*

Try this handy checklist to build your LinkedIn profile.

LINKEDIN PROFILE BUILDER

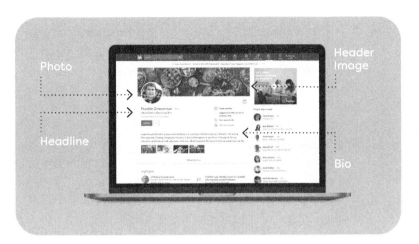

Photo

- ❏ Smiling
- ❏ Well-lit
- ❏ Professional (but not stale)
- ❏ Clear view of your face
- ❏ You are the main focus

Header image

- ❏ Related to your profession
- ❏ Works in panoramic format
- ❏ Visually interesting
- ❏ Complements profile photo

Headline

- ❏ Clear and concise
- ❏ Feels grounded
- ❏ Highlights the problems you solve

Bio

- ❏ Succinct as possible
- ❏ Highlights the key problems you solve
- ❏ Retains a professional feel
- ❏ Feels human (not just cold facts)
- ❏ Doesn't read like a résumé

Other profile tips

- ❏ All fields up-to-date
- ❏ Full job and education history
- ❏ More complete, the better
- ❏ Avoid sounding like a job hunter

ACTION POINTS

~~~

1. **Invest the time.** The right looking profile encourages more prospects to connect. More connected prospects equal more opportunities to generate leads.
2. **Don't be bland.** Never be afraid to show some of your personality in your profile. It helps you to stand out and feel more approachable.
3. **Use top-quality photos.** Make sure your face is clearly visible, and that you look happy. People gravitate towards cheerful individuals.
4. **Keep your profile current.** Don't leave people questioning what you do or the experience you have.
5. **Be the expert.** Write articles and get recommendations to present expertise. Make sure that prospects know you are the real deal.
6. **Use the Wonder Leads Profile Builder** to keep your profile up-to-scratch.

6

Building Your Connections

solating the correct decision-maker in a company can be complicated. In fact, the term 'decision-maker' is usually a bit of a misnomer. Yes, there is often one person with a hand on the purse strings who can greenlight the project or services you sell, but that's not before they have had the help of several teams across their organisation. All of these additional people are going to give varying degrees of input as to whether what your business sells presents fair value for money.

Insight from America suggests that the number of decision-makers involved in B2B purchases has increased by more than 20 per cent in the space of just two years. The additional input comes from a wide variety of positions, locations and teams, resulting in greater risk aversion and decision paralysis.[1]

To a B2B professional, this probably sounds depressingly familiar: people finding increasing ways to pick holes in your sales proposition. It's frustrating, but the reality: layers of bureaucracy and the reluctance or general inability of anyone to take individual responsibility become more deeply entrenched, the larger an organisation gets.

Still, this presents a rather exciting opportunity when lining up prospects for our Wonder Leads. Instead of just having to rely on one person replying at one organisation, more often than not there will be multiple avenues of entry via different people in different positions. All of these people can influence the purchasing decision to a varying degree – and that is something you can, and should, use to your advantage.

Don't underestimate the value of specifying precisely the type of businesses and people you want to contact: of course, this is insanely obvious but worth highlighting nonetheless, as it's incredibly important. I've been in so many marketing meetings where the organisation has absolutely no idea who their intended audience is. It seems to be an especially nasty epidemic in the public sector, where responses such as "What do you mean, *who* is this is for? We want this campaign to target *everyone* of course!", seem to be an everyday occurrence.

The problem is, it's impossible to target *everyone* because *everyone* is different. Everyone has different hates and loves, dreams and nightmares. If we were to pick two random people from the street and ask what makes them happy, drives them or makes them angry, what are the chances of getting two identical answers? Very slim. The values that everybody holds, and the priority they place on those values, changes from person-to-person.

It goes without saying that there will be some crossover of values too, as this is a natural part of life. People who share similar outlooks choose to partner up, join the same teams or campaign against the same issues. They choose to join one company over another for the same reason, because at their heart, that's all companies are: collections of people who share similar values.

> *The trick is finding the companies most likely to see the most value in what you and your business can provide.*

Identifying prospects

Wonder Leads is all about maximising the impact of a relatively small number of approaches. To achieve that, it's important to play to your strengths. The following steps will help to achieve just that.

1. WHAT IS YOUR MARKET SECTOR?

In which markets do you have the most reliable track record of success? It could be a single industry, or span multiple market sectors. You just need to be confident that your case studies and value proposition will get the attention of other businesses in that sector.

2. WHO DO YOU SERVE BEST?

Are they a specific size? What about turnover, location? These might seem arbitrary questions, but they will help you quickly identify the most promising opportunities, once your search is underway.

3. WHO ARE THE DECISION-MAKERS?

Draw on your experience of previous purchasing scenarios: who were the key decision-makers in charge of procuring your product or service? What other type of job roles are likely to influence those people in deciding to buy from you or not?

Your goal here is to look beyond the obvious for additional avenues of entry, should your ideal contact not be an active LinkedIn user.

Try the Prospect Identifier Matrix to build a picture of who to approach.

PROSPECT IDENTIFIER MATRIX

	1st choice	2nd choice	3rd choice
Industry			
Position			
Location			
Turnover			
Employees			

Prospect Identifier matrix example

	1st choice	2nd choice	3rd choice
Industry	Food and drink	Fast-moving consumer goods	Pharmaceutical
Position	Chief marketing officer	Marketing director	Marketing manager
Location	London	South East	England
Turnover	£100m+	£50m+	£10m+
Employees	500+	250+	100+

4. WHAT ARE YOUR SALES TRIGGERS?

Sales triggers are events and situations within businesses that often correspond to new sales opportunities. If you haven't defined yours already, then a great place to start is looking back at past sales conversations. What motivated those customers to contact you? What were their immediate problems needing support from a business like yours: maybe a change of leadership, merger or PR emergency?

There will be many such events presenting an ideal chance for your business to help a potential customer overcome some of their challenges. If you're clued up on what yours are, then you'll be able to identify an excellent introduction opportunity when one comes around.

This handy checklist can help you identify common sales triggers for your business.

COMMON B2B
SALES TRIGGERS

Financial

- ❑ Management buyout
- ❑ Additional funding
- ❑ Initial Public Offering (IPO) or stock market listing
- ❑ Quarterly results
- ❑ Poor financial results
- ❑ Change of prices
- ❑ Entering administration

Operations

- ❑ Disruptive new technology
- ❑ Mergers and acquisitions
- ❑ Large customer acquisition
- ❑ Change of availability in materials
- ❑ Relocation
- ❑ Supplier difficulties
- ❑ Time pressures
- ❑ Equipment failure
- ❑ Seasonal changes

Legal

- ❑ New patents
- ❑ Data breaches
- ❑ Legal difficulties
- ❑ Legislation changes
- ❑ Contract expirations

Strategic

- ❑ Expansion
- ❑ Entering new markets
- ❑ Change of business strategy
- ❑ Major competitive moves
- ❑ CEO announcement in annual report

People

- ❑ New executives
- ❑ Lay-off and redundancy
- ❑ Change of jobs
- ❑ New board members
- ❑ Rapid hiring

Marketing

- ❑ Awards
- ❑ New website
- ❑ New marketing or advertising
- ❑ PR announcements
- ❑ Event attendance
- ❑ Rebranding

Other

- ❑ Seasonal
- ❑ Industry-specific
- ❑ Trends

ACTION POINTS

~~~

1. **Play to your strengths**. Concentrate on customer groups where you have the best track record of success, as prospects relate to positive examples.
2. **Focus.** The more you concentrate your attention on a narrow group of prospects, the more valuable the connections you can create.
3. **Think beyond the primary decision-maker**. Less obvious job roles can be highly influential in the buying process and are worth contacting, especially if you can't connect to the primary target.
4. **Note your sales triggers**. This makes it easier to identify and prioritise the people you want to target.
5. **Use the Wonder Leads Prospect Identifier Matrix** to help you isolate and prioritise your prospects. Focus on the best fits before expanding your search.

Finding prospects

With more than 500 million members, it's pretty safe to assume there are plenty of people who meet your new target profiles on Linke-dIn. Like any humongous database, the real trouble is finding them. Thankfully, several tools and techniques are available to help zero in on the right people.

1. LINKEDIN SEARCH

The first and most commonly used way of finding new connections is the primary LinkedIn search tool. You'll be pleased to know that LinkedIn has an entire library of up-to-date help documentation available for every aspect of its platform, including Searching (linkedin.com/help). The following gives a few general pointers on using those search functions to save valuable time.

Leverage your existing network first

You can do this easily just by checking through your existing connections, as a time-saving and common-sense exercise. There's a good chance that your connections will know people in similar positions at other companies: after all, everyone has a job history, and people within industries tend to stick together. If those connections are clients and you've done good work for them, these shared connections might have seen your profile appear in their feed; they might even have heard your customers saying positive things about you.

People are far more likely to connect if they recognise shared connections, interests and positive experiences.

Here are some useful things to consider when searching within your network.

Use the 'People' search function

By searching within 'People' and using the handy 'All Filters' function, it's possible to run a focused search purely within a current connection's network – which makes it easy to quickly find people by job title, company and location.

Focus on second-degree connections

These are the direct contacts to your first-degree connections being searched, which means a much higher chance of using their relationship to your advantage.

Don't forget about suppliers and partners

You aren't limited to searching within customer networks: suppliers and trade partners can be an equally rich source of potential connections, because they inhabit the same world.

The importance of influencers

Industry influencers are highly active on LinkedIn within a particular target sector: they might be bloggers, journalists, speakers or network managers. The chances are, they'll have a lot of connections to people and companies of interest. Connecting with influencers makes it possible to search their network and extend your own, which can open up doors.

Expand your search thoughtfully

Once your existing connections have been exhausted, searches can be expanded to companies and individuals outside of your network. That might be via the search function, or through account activity visible in your feed. Connecting with people as a result of feed activity can be doubly beneficial, because it proves that the individual is an active LinkedIn user: it makes them a safer bet for targeting later.

If you've been a LinkedIn user for any length of time, no doubt you will have come across the 'People You May Know' feature (usually viewable under 'My Network'). This needs to be handled delicately, because pressing the 'connect' button fires off an anonymous request. That's a really bad idea (as we will discuss in Chapter 7), but the feature can throw up some interesting connections, so it might be worth using. Just make sure you click into the suggested person's profile and send a connection request the usual way, rather than using the 'Connect' button in the list of recommendations. It takes a bit longer, but it's worth it.

A quick word of warning on searching: LinkedIn imposes limits on the number of searches and profile views which users can carry out each month on a free account. LinkedIn views too much of this behaviour as an indication of recruitment or lead-generation activity, arguing that it qualifies as paid commercial activity – and it's difficult to argue with that position. The frustrating part is that LinkedIn doesn't publish what these limits are, or how it calculates them. For our purposes, just know that this limitation exists.

Why does this matter? The Wonder Leads methodology engages in a fair amount of searching and profile viewing, which means you might need to upgrade to a paid plan where you won't find yourself restricted by the level of searching activity. While additional expense is never welcome, LinkedIn does provide some extra tools to play with which might come in handy. Let's look at the two main ones next.

2. LINKEDIN PREMIUM

This is the basic paid account for individual users, which comes in a range of options depending on your needs. At the time of writing, the cheapest plan offering unlimited people browsing is Premium Business, which costs just under £42 a month (around $55). Premium plans have a range of benefits, the most notable of which is the ability to send InMail.

InMail

InMail allows you to send direct messages to anyone on LinkedIn. While this may sound tempting, there is no benefit in using InMail as part of the Wonder Leads process, because spammers frequently abuse InMail for bulk sales approaches. For that reason, I ignore the vast majority of InMail that comes my way (and I'm sure many others do the same).

> *Your goal is to build a connection that allows you to engage in meaningful conversation.*

For this reason, stick to good, old-fashioned connection requests. If there is someone you want to contact outside of your third-degree connections, try and find another way to connect with them, or move on to someone new. There are plenty more fish in the sea.

3. SALES NAVIGATOR

Sales Navigator gives you access to a whole host of sales-related tools, including a much more advanced version of the primary LinkedIn search facility. It enables searches which can drill down to any company or user across the platform and from there, issue connection requests.

Using Sales Navigator, it's possible to build lists of targets by segmenting people into different job roles or industries. It tracks activity on the people and companies you want to follow, alerting you if, for example, a prospect moves into a new role or features in a news article for winning an award. All interesting information which can be put to good use later in the process.

Other useful features include search alerts which email you lead opportunities that match preferred industry or job titles – this can save time hunting for the right connections. Sales Navigator also comes with a much more insightful organisation view, displaying all the LinkedIn users connected to a business: a huge time saver when there are multiple potential targets at a single organisation.

The downside to Sales Navigator is the cost: starting at roughly double the price of Linked Premium Business. It's by no means essential, as the basic LinkedIn search might be perfectly adequate and a Premium account offers plenty of useful features. Still, I have personally found Sales Navigator to be a handy tool worth the additional investment because of the time it saves.

ACTION POINTS

1. **Start closest to home.** Prospects are more likely to connect with you if you share common connections, which makes the process more efficient.
2. **Search beyond your customer networks.** Suppliers, partners and influencers can all provide valuable routes to your ideal prospects.
3. **Avoid shortcuts.** Always send a connection note, and avoid InMail to maximise your chances of connecting.
4. **Start for free.** Use the standard built-in search tools within LinkedIn, then move to a paid solution only if you need more functionality.

7

Reaching Out to Prospects

At the risk of stating the blindingly obvious, the golden rule of connection messages is: always use one. (I know, I'm a genius...) I feel compelled to point this out because even now, despite the volume of advice that exists warning LinkedIn users against sending anonymous connection requests, a high percentage *still* appear in my inbox every week. Guess what happens to every one of those requests: they get deleted straightaway. If someone can't even spend 30 seconds to use my name and tell me why they want to connect, I can't possibly imagine what value they think they will add to my network.

Your connection message

Thankfully, it's precisely because there are so many lazy people in the world that your Wonder Leads approach is going to stand you in good stead – because you will be including a carefully constructed connection *Note*. There isn't much wiggle room here: a LinkedIn Note is minimal, currently just 299 characters, which leaves little option but to keep things brief.

The message content is crucial, as a connection Note is likely to be the very first direct contact we make with a prospect. Of course, we already know that charging in with all the grace of a gung-ho gibbon is not the way to go:

"I'm Dave from Big Co., and we are the business you've been dreaming about. We have this insane new product that is guaranteed to change your fortunes. Come on, let's connect!"

You know as well as I do that this type of thing really doesn't win anyone any friends. The only thing it does achieve is a painfully high rejection percentage, and several black 'spam' marks against the sender's account. Can you imagine someone coming up to you in the office and saying something like that – would you give them the time of day? Unless you're short of friends or desperate to do anything to avoid filing that blasted report you've promised, the answer is going to be a categoric 'No'.

Structuring a message with politeness is essential to start building positive connections with other people.[1] Curt, perfunctory words may save some time and generate some peripheral results, but they never lay the foundations for building meaningful relationships. Practising politeness requires significantly more time because it demands empathy, and empathy does wonders for the way we are perceived: it solidifies the social bond.

With that in mind, let's look at some helpful pointers when constructing a connection message.

1. STICK TO THE BASICS

Again, this will be really obvious, but just include a friendly 'Hello' and address your contact correctly by name. Introduce yourself, but avoid overstepping the mark. Do ask them for permission to connect – they'll appreciate the courtesy.

2. DON'T SELL

At this stage, you haven't built up the social currency to start asking for anything other than permission to be part of your prospect's network, which is a big ask in itself. If fortune smiles, they will say 'Yes'. Trying to sell in the connection Note is like trying to row across the Atlantic in a leaky canoe: it expends a lot of energy and might seem like it's going somewhere, but sooner or later, that approach is going down.

3. USE YOUR LEVERAGE

Perhaps you share a close connection with the prospect, or have met briefly at an event? Maybe someone recommended you get in touch? Whatever it might be, so long as it is genuine, it's fine not to be afraid to tailor your template message to the individual. This will significantly improve your chances of overall success (as we'll see later on in Chapter 9, 'Personalise whenever you can').

Try out the Connection Message Template to help construct your note.

CONNECTION MESSAGE TEMPLATE

Hello [NAME],

I am the [JOB TITLE] at a [TYPE OF BUSINESS] based in [LOCATION] called [BUSINESS NAME]. We specialise in helping [INDUSTRY/MARKET] to [CORE VALUE]. Would you be happy to connect?

[CLOSE]

[YOUR FIRST NAME]

Example 1: Cold connection (246 characters)

Hello Sophie,

I am the owner at a large-format print company based in London called BigPrint. We specialise in offering white-label services to PR agencies working with hospitality clients. I wondered if you might be happy to connect?

Regards,

Wendy

Example 2: Shared experience (215 characters)

Hello Lin,

I saw your talk at the international expo last week and thought it was excellent. I notice we share several contacts between our networks and wondered if you might be happy to connect?

Many thanks,

Jackson

Example 3: Mutual connection (244 characters)

Hello Eric,

I met your colleague Anita at the employment networking event last week, and we briefly discussed our HR policy writing service. She suggested you might be the best person to contact. Would you be happy to connect?

Kind regards,

Louisa

Example 4: Activity feed (250 characters)

Hello Gill,

I came across your post on improving workplace efficiency and thought you made some excellent points, especially the one about streamlining IT operations! I thought I'd get in touch to see if you might be happy to connect?

Kind regards,

Alan

ACTION POINTS

~~~

1. **Be polite.** Politeness demonstrates empathy, and empathy builds relationships.
2. **Concentrate on the value you deliver.** Selling turns people off. Instead, help people to understand the strengths you can bring as a connection.
3. **Use your inside knowledge.** Personalising your connection message with salient details helps you to stand out as an individual.
4. **Use the Wonder Leads Connection Message Template** to help structure your message in the right way for success.

Handling responses

It's almost impossible to connect successfully every time with a cold prospect. Just knowing that will help your ego to survive this process intact! There are a million reasons why connections won't be accepted. The recipient might:

- Not be an active LinkedIn user
- Have misinterpreted the message
- Have had terrible experiences with similar-sounding companies before
- Be inundated with connection requests, and simply missed this one
- Reserve their network for a select group – for example, only people they have met face-to-face

(Then of course, there is always the unfortunate possibility that they simply don't like the look of our face. I prefer not to dwell on that final scenario, if only to save my fragile self-esteem from taking any further beatings...) Nevertheless, I'm sure you appreciate the point: we simply can't legislate for every response that does or doesn't arrive.

The statistics on connection acceptances are pretty varied. Some claim acceptance rates of up to 80 per cent:[2] in other words, every 100 connection requests generates nearly 80 new connections. That seems exceptionally optimistic – especially given that nearly half of LinkedIn members are classed as inactive.[3] With this in mind, a 30–50 per cent acceptance rate is a better goal, particularly as we'll be reaching out to cold prospects.

CONNECTION REQUEST LIMITS

While we're on the subject of statistics, there is some additional information to be aware of relating to acceptance rates. LinkedIn imposes a limit on the number of connection requests that users can make: at the time of writing, it's 3,000. This might sound like plenty, but running a full-time Wonder Leads programme may mean finding that limit looming faster than we realise. Although LinkedIn has never restricted my account, it does happen: if you exceed your quota, you may find your account is limited and yourself unable to send any further requests.

If this happens to you, don't worry. The restriction facility seems to be there primarily to stop spammers sending large volumes of connection requests over a short period. Because Wonder Leads is a 'less-is-more' approach, it's doubtful that you will fit this profile. If you do hit the limit, you can ask LinkedIn to lift the restriction on your account via the page in their help section. If you can demonstrate that you're making legitimate approaches and have a decent acceptance rate, you have a higher-than-average chance of being unblocked. After all, it is firmly in LinkedIn's interests to keep you active on its platform. Hopefully, knowing this should give you another strong incentive to micro-target prospects, and ensure that connection requests are as brilliant as they possibly can be.

ACTION POINTS

1. **Non-response is normal.** Half (if not more) of all LinkedIn members are not regular users.
2. **Treat responses as a learning exercise.** Don't be afraid to tailor your messages according to the success and feedback you receive.
3. **Get advice.** For additional validation, ask colleagues or friends to critique your connection message.
4. **Target quick responders.** The people who accept your requests most quickly are often the most active users, and the best ones on which to focus your efforts.
5. **Don't send a reply, even if you get one.** That would undermine the impact of your main Wonder Leads introduction.

Now you have the tools to start building your network, it's time to get your prospects excited about the value you bring to the table. It's time to start telling your story.

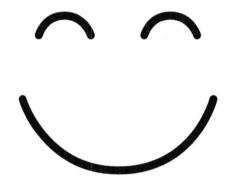

PART
IV

STORYTELLING

73

8

Why Storytelling Matters

Storytelling is as old as speech. For thousands of years, humans have used this method to share their experiences of the world around them and pass on information from one generation to the next.

One of the oldest examples of storytelling lies in the Chauvet Cave in France. Inside it is a vivid depiction of a volcanic eruption which must have had major significance to the individuals who painted it, given the painstaking methods it took to create it. Scientists have dated the Upper Palaeolithic artwork at around 30,000 years old; further examples are earlier still, such as the painting of wild cattle, dated at about 40,000 years old discovered in a cave in East Kalimantan, Borneo.

"OK Dave, that's all very interesting – but how does cave art relate to generating leads?"

Good question. Clearly, this is not a history book, but it is examining how humans interact successfully with one another. Stories have always had – and continue to have – a vital role in building stronger relationships between people. Indeed, the significance of storytelling as way of communicating is evangelised by everyone from the world's most influential screenwriting lecturer, Robert McKee,[1] to arguably its most influential marketer, Seth Godin.[2] (And that applies *everywhere*, even the B2B sales world.).

In the case of Wonder Leads, our story is told through the script we use to deliver our video introductions. It allows control of the narrative and with it, perception of us and our business. Any business possessing a strong brand and a clearly defined positioning statement is at a distinct advantage here. Why? Because the whole reason for building a brand is to help articulate unique value to the outside world.

A great brand can clearly explain:

- What type of problems it solves
- What group of customers it serves
- Why it's different from the competition

In other words, a great brand tells people *why* a business matters.

If your business has a strong brand, you should be a long way down the road already to crafting a genuinely compelling script. If you don't, then fear not: creating an engaging story for your business is not as complicated as it might seem. It simply requires knowing how to piece it together.

Preparing your story outline

Before you start working on the text for your Wonder Leads story, it's good just to take a moment to step back and consider the broader outline of the process, so as to understand your prospect's journey.

Wonder Leads has been designed to complement the B2B *Buying* process. That might seem odd when we're adopting a proactive business development approach. "Surely a B2B *Sales* process would be more appropriate?" you ask.

Well, no. As we identified at the start of this book, *the primary purpose of a Wonder Leads approach is to plant the seed of interest in a prospect.* You should never deliver one with the expectation of winning an immediate sale. Seeds grow and bear fruit whenever the recipient says the time is right, not when we do – it might be weeks, months or even years into the future. It all depends on circumstances and the frequency of the purchasing window in which a business operates. The key is doing everything possible to influence your recipient's *purchasing* process, so when the time to buy does arrive, you are at the front of their mind.

I have written at length about the B2B buying process and how to influence it in a white paper, 'Engineering Customers' (Figure 1).[3] Every buyer goes through four steps when they intend to procure a new B2B service:

1. Searching
2. Filtering
3. Assessing
4. Selecting.

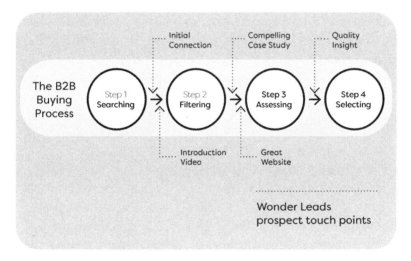

Figure 1: Prospect journey map

STEP 1: SEARCHING

The first parts of the Wonder Leads journey are the connection script and introduction video. The script creates the connection, then the video turns it into something more meaningful. These two steps intercept your prospects' normal searching process: the point at which buyers are actively looking for new suppliers.

Getting on a buyer's radar ahead of their *Searching* process is the perfect start, but it takes a lot more to survive the *Filtering* process.

....

STEP 2: FILTERING

During *Filtering*, the buyer decides which companies are worth further consideration. The novel approach of a Wonder Leads video should stand you in good stead here, but a great video alone isn't enough to make it through a thorough filtering process. Everyone knows that words are cheap, and that buyers have too many options and far too much information at their fingertips to be persuaded by empty promises. Statements need to be backed up with substance.

The central part of your new story will be an *online case study* to demonstrate the real impact of your work. The case study should sit on your company website and be as good as you can possibly make it, featuring:

- Well-written copy
- Great pictures
- Descriptions of the challenges you helped the client overcome
- Testimonials from your client
- The value you delivered

The value might be financial, efficiency or any other improvement metric relevant to what your business does: it just needs to be quantifiable, genuine and as attention-grabbing as possible.

Ideally, the focus of the case study should be a well-known customer with whom the prospect might be familiar, as this gives your case study more weight. If that isn't an option, just use your strongest case study for any client.

> *It's better to have a strong case study that shows excellent results for a less well-known customer, than it is to feature a household name where the impact of your work is less obvious.*

If you already have a case study like this, great! You're well ahead of the game. If you don't, it will take a little more time and effort to create a new one, but nothing will do more to establish the credibility of your business.

This is also the perfect time to carry out a customer-orientated audit of your website. Once prospects start landing on a website, the chances are that some them will do a bit of exploring. I have worked on a lot of websites over the years, and it still pains me to see how little effort many companies put into their online presence.

> *A website is the most critical tool in any business's marketing toolkit: it's all that most people will ever see or know about a business.*

A website needs to accurately reflect the quality of the work that its company does, to make the right impression on visitors. If its design, content or structure are under par, visitors will be left with a poor impression of the business. The good news is that all these things can be easily addressed with the right support.

The effort you put into improving your online presence will pay you back tenfold.

STEP 3: ASSESSING

A great case study and professional website should go a long way to helping you navigate the *Filtering* process. From there, the *Assessing* process begins, when prospects start shortlisting the most suitable suppliers from the options available. *Assessing* is an extremely complex process, primarily driven by the buyer's most pressing concerns. And they aren't looking for reasons to do business with a company; they're looking for every reason *not* to.

'Buyer's remorse' is a hugely significant factor in all purchase decisions. People are more afraid of the thought of getting a decision wrong and having it come back to bite them, than they are excited by the idea of getting it right and the benefits that might follow. This is why people always hesitate before buying that new car, choosing a builder to work on their house or commissioning a consultancy to develop a new software package.

It is during the *Assessing* process of the B2B buying process that many companies fall by the wayside. *They may be capable of delivering incredible value, but they're unable to articulate that value clearly enough.* As we've already identified, instead of building reassurance through the way they communicate to the outside world (their marketing), they leave room for doubt by presenting themselves poorly or failing to provide sufficient evidence of their capabilities.

While this might sound superficial, it isn't at all. Unless a buyer has purchased from a company before, all they have to judge the company on is the way it communicates. They use the company's marketing to construct an imaginary picture of a world where they are a customer of that business: if that image isn't as picturesque as the one they expect, they will move on and look for other suppliers who can paint something more compelling.

This is why it is vitally important to build as much equity into your knowledge and abilities as possible. Doing so helps to present a brighter, safer image of you as someone who brings value to the table by solving complex problems. The best way to achieve that is through education and sharing *insight*.

The reason is three-fold:

1. **Elevates your business** – quality insight raises a business above the pool of mediocrity defining most operations in any sector
2. **Clarifies your value proposition** – sharing insight positions a company's value in a way that the prospect can easily understand

3. **Provides viral content** – prospects can easily share insight between colleagues. Because multiple decision-makers are involved in the majority of B2B sales, insight makes it possible to align all stakeholders with a single way of thinking.

A quality insight piece should be the final part of your Wonder Leads journey. Again, if you already have something ready-made, great. If not, we aren't talking *War and Peace* or a doctoral thesis! A terrific insight piece can take many forms:

- How-to guides
- Surveys
- Online analysis and feedback
- White papers
- Ebooks
- Infographics
- Seminars

The only requirement is providing genuine value directly related to your area of business that is not readily available elsewhere.

If creating insight content is new to you and your business, it can feel a little daunting. "What would anyone possibly have to learn from me?" is a relatively common response. Everyone has something useful to share, so don't be concerned! After all, if your prospect knew everything you do, why would they need to buy from a company like yours in the first place? (*The Challenger Sale*[4] and the follow-up, *The Challenger Customer*[5] by Matthew Dixon and Brent Adamson are both fantastic reads for anyone keen to find out more about the reasons and methods for creating B2B insight.)

If you want to get a head start, the Wonder Leads Insight Idea Matrix below will get your ideas flowing and help you identify suitable insight opportunities, based on your available time and resources.

INSIGHT IDEA MATRIX

What is our ultimate objective?

Who are we targeting?

What is our angle?

	Idea 1	Idea 2	Idea 3
Format:			
What's the main aim?			
Why is it useful to prospects?			
It has authority because:			
What do we need?			
Timeline			

Insight Idea Matrix Example

What is our ultimate objective?

Generate free trials for Product X

Who are we targeting?

Technical managers

What is our angle?

	Idea 1	Idea 2	Idea 3
Format:	White paper	Book	Online test
What's the main aim?	Demonstrates the true scale of wasted productivity by companies which don't have access to the increased efficiency offered by Product X	Demonstrates our breadth of knowledge in productivity improvement measures	Allows prospects to quickly gain an understanding of estimated and avoidable financial losses for their own business through implementing a system like Product X
Why is it useful to prospects?	Opens readers' eyes to a problem that they are unlikely to be aware of, which and could make a big difference to the bottom line	Provides a go-to resource for anyone interested in improving productivity within their environment	Gains immediate assessment of current lost productivity without having to engage in a sales conversation upfront
It has authority because:	Features views from our CEO Features insight from existing leading industry sources Commissions a survey of companies to provide analysis and insight on the results	Uses all our senior leaders' expertise and knowledge Provides real-life examples that back up the statements we make	The results are accurate and based on live, captured data Indicates where the analysis has come from Provides access to a data sample as required Underestimates results to avoid overpromising
What do we need?	Someone to collect the research Interview the CEO Someone to write the content Someone to design the white paper Short print run Form to download PDF from our website Social media ads promoting content	Researchers to interview all senior team leaders Professional writer Typesetter/designer Printing Form to request a copy Promo adverts	Plan data and analysis Write answers Design interface Develop test functionality Integrate with our website Promo adverts
Timeline	8 weeks	6 months	4 weeks

In an ideal world, the insight piece should be created before moving on to filming and subsequent stages of the process, but the insight piece is bonus content as far as your prospect is concerned. They won't be expecting it, which means it won't matter too much if it's a few weeks, or even a few months, behind the optimum schedule (we'll be looking at this further in Chapter 17). Whatever you do, don't rush out poor quality insight just to have anything to send out due to an arbitrary deadline, as this only undermines the whole approach. It's more imperative for the insight piece to offer genuine value, so that when the time does come to share, it truly enlightens your audience.

STEP 4: SELECTING

In the context of inbound B2B sales, *Selecting* is the process that prospects go through to decide who they want to work with, after they've contacted the companies assessed as being the most suitable. This phase is driven largely by the quality of the sales process. Wonder Leads is a framework for generating leads rather than closing deals, which is outside the scope of this book. (If you're interested in learning more about how to influence this final stage, my ebook 'Engineering Customers' will help to explain further.)

ACTION POINTS

1. **Plan the journey.** Understand exactly what steps you want your prospect to take, and how and where they fit into the B2B buying process.
2. **Prepare a compelling case study.** Don't just focus on what you did for your customer. Include tangible evidence of the difference you made to their business.
3. **Showcase your knowledge through valuable insight.** Positioning yourself as an expert reinforces the quality of your initial approach and marks you out as a person of genuine value.
4. **Audit your online presence.** Once you have people visiting your website, make sure it's good enough to keep them interested in what you do and drive further action.
5. **Use the Wonder Leads Insight Idea Matrix** to help you develop concepts for engaging, educational and practical insight pieces.

9

Building a Wonder Leads Script

The script for a Wonder Leads video forms the backbone of the entire process. It sets the tone of communication, and controls the actions a prospect is expected to take. Without a compelling script, it will be a struggle to make the level of connection necessary to generate genuine sales opportunities. If you aren't a natural writer, the following steps will walk you through building a compelling script for your business.

The eight golden rules of scriptwriting

You'll be telling your story through your video script, so it needs to be a positive one that not only shows respect and friendliness, but offers genuine value to the prospect. A great script puts consideration of the prospect front and centre, otherwise it risks losing impact.

------

1. Be courteous
The principles that apply to building a connection message also apply to your script, except the significance is tenfold. Because you will be alone on-camera, what you say will be under the microscope, so respect is the order of the day.

2. Keep it simple

Your prospects may not be as knowledgeable about your field, so it's best not to confuse things by using jargon or technical terms. Avoid going into excessive detail about what you do; instead, it's fine just to focus on the main problems you can solve for them.

3. Demonstrate real value

The value that your business delivers needs to be crystal clear: a message can find itself diluted by too many features and benefits, so just focus on your ability to solve your prospects' pain points. They might be blissfully unaware that they have a problem at all.

4. Be cheerful

Try to brighten the prospect's day by being happy and focusing on the positive things you can deliver. Definitely avoid running down your competitors, as this gives a negative impression of both you and your business.

5. Keep your first draft under 240 words

For your first draft, it's best to use a computer programme in which you can track word count: for example, Microsoft Word, Google Docs or Open Office. The draft needs to be under 240 words because of timing when delivered to camera.

6. Speak it normally in under 2 minutes

Your prospect is going to be busy, so it's sensible not to take up any more of their time than absolutely necessary – otherwise you risk losing their interest. Aim to deliver the script in your average talking speed in under 2 minutes (ideally, less than 90 seconds).

7. Treat every word like the 'enemy'

It pays to be ruthless with editing. Imagine you are being paid £100 for every unnecessary word you remove in your script: this will help to make it shorter, punchier and infinitely more effective.

8. Make it feel personal

Your new script is going to get a lot of use, so it's key to be 100 per cent comfortable with every word. If you read it aloud and something doesn't flow naturally, it's a good sign that further tweaking is required. Taking the time to fine-tune the narrative will make a big difference to the ease, quality and fluency of your delivery.

Constructing your script

Although you've sent a connection message and your prospect has accepted, this is still the beginning of your relationship. Turning that connection into something meaningful is to win them over at a personal level.

1. LEAD WITH A GREETING

Starting with a simple 'Hello' – the universally recognised greeting first brought into everyday use in 1927 by Thomas Edison on the invention of his telephone – is a pretty safe bet for starting your next conversation on a positive note. Equally, you could opt for 'Good morning', 'Good afternoon' or 'Hi', depending on your personal preference. Just check that it's polite, appropriate and feels natural for you.

Say their name

If you want to get people on-side, there's no better way than to follow up by using your prospect's name. Even at the beginning of the last century, leading thinkers in the world of professional development such as Dale Carnegie recognised the positive reaction this bestows on a person when you use their name.[1] We now know the scientific reasons behind this.

According to a 2006 research report published in the journal *Brain Research*,[2] hearing your first name (versus hearing someone else's) causes an unusual reaction in the brain. It's the reason why you don't bat an eyelid if a random person shouts someone else's name across a busy train station, but if they shout yours, you immediately react and focus on the source.

Using the prospect's name right at the start helps to build that all-important personal connection. Significantly, they will grasp within the first two seconds that the content they are watching has been crafted *especially for them*. The power that such an instant realisation has on the impact of a message, and the recipient's willingness to watch the remaining video, can't be underestimated. You can strengthen this impact even more by dropping in the name of their company.

Say 'thank you'

The next task is to ensure they understand the reason for the video. Even though the steps you've taken this far will have spurred their interest, the chances are that your recipient might still feel a bit guarded. We're all so inundated by sales approaches that when anyone new contacts us, the natural reaction is cynicism. (Or, if you live in Yorkshire, extreme cynicism!)

Instead, put the recipient at ease so that they can listen to the rest of your short message without fear of the hard sell. This video is an opportunity to thank your newly-acquired contact for letting you into their world, so do let them know that you're grateful for being connected.

Show empathy

The next goal is to get the prospect's permission to keep talking. Remember, prospects will be short of time, so the objective is to let them know that the window they're granting by watching this video isn't going to be abused. It's good practice to explain that it will only be a short video, and to apologise for taking up their time. This demonstrates empathy and respect – the two things we've already identified as essential to relationship-building.

Be an educator

The final part of our opening should make it abundantly clear that the purpose of the video is *education*, not *selling*. This is probably a good time to highlight the subtle difference between the two. Both involve winning the other person around to a viewpoint: if done well, they close the sale; if not, the deal is lost – but that's where the similarity ends.

Selling is selfishly motivated. It uses all the knowledge, tools and information at a seller's disposal to drive a prospect towards the end goal: breaking down their opposition and closing the sale. There is little room for disagreement or diversion, because that means delaying or abandoning the seller's objectives. Selling has a place (although I am struggling to think where that could be in this day and age), but it is *not* within Wonder Leads.

Education requires adopting a far more useful mindset. A great educator goes into a conversation knowing that end goals are meaningless, and the use of force, futile. While they might believe strongly in their own thought process, they appreciate that the other person might hold their own, opposing beliefs in equally high esteem – so the educator concentrates all their energy on the *way* they structure the argument. If the argument is strong, the other person *might* align with their way of thinking; but the educator never *presumes* this will be the case. They always leave space for disagreement, because they understand that it's a natural part of any conversation.

> *When the other person feels empowered to disagree, the educator knows that they are far more likely to play an active role in the discussion.*

Let's break this down. Say you're writing a message for a cold prospect – you won't know:

- The real situation within their business
- What relationships they might have with existing suppliers
- The pressures they might be under personally
- Their immediate priorities

Trying to force a sale in such circumstances would be like trying to reach Mars with nothing but an elastic band and an empty water bottle! Instead, adopting an educator mindset acknowledges the fact that, despite the seemingly limitless strengths of the argument being put before them, the prospect is unlikely to give two hoots – and that's perfectly OK. Giving your prospect the freedom to interpret a message on their own terms not only focuses your mind on the quality of the argument being delivered, but simultaneously gains their respect.

> *In the long run, this delivers far more dividends than any sale derived by force of will.*

Put it all together

The final step is to pull these elements into a robust opening statement. For example:

> "Hello George,
> I just wanted to say thank you for connecting. I hope I might be able to take a minute of your time to quickly introduce Supplier Co., in case we might be of use to you and Prospect Co. at some point in the future."

2. PROVIDE SOME BACKGROUND

Now the prospect understands your reason for sending the video, it's time to start telling your story. That means explaining what your business is and, most importantly, *why* it matters – and it's much trickier than it sounds, especially when time is in short supply.

If you ask any company what they do, they should be able to tell you. "We're designers", "We're lawyers", "We're builders": describing the profession is everyone's default response, but it's simply a description of *what* they do. The problem arises when someone replies, "OK, so what?" Unless a business exists in a glorious vacuum, it's likely to be one of many potential suppliers on offer.

We've already identified that to get a prospect's attention, a business must be able to articulate how it is different in a way that matters to them: and this is where many companies come unstuck. Trying to articulate why you are different, better, why you matter, demands that you understand the real value your business offers to the market, and which groups of customers will appreciate it the most (as we touched on in Chapter 8).[3] This defines and builds a brand, and it's the reason why businesses with the most powerful brands dominate markets.

A business that has already been through a brand strategy process to define what it is and why it matters will already have this written down in a brand positioning statement: you can use this as a perfect introduction to your business, albeit with some minor adjustments so it can be spoken more naturally.

If you don't have a statement or are unlikely to get access to one any time soon, no problem! The following three-step shortcut will help you formulate one that works for a Wonder Leads script.

Describe your business

First, write down a one to three-word description of your business: for example, 'strategic marketing agency', 'bookkeepers', 'chartered surveyors'.

Define your industry specialism

Next, write down which segment of customers you can best serve: for example, 'hoteliers', 'beauty salons', or 'Microsoft dynamics developers'. Try to be as focused and specific as you can: aim it at the smallest possible group of customers on whom you can build a sustainable business. Focusing your attention on a tighter, core section of customers helps your business to stand out from the flock of generalists who dominate most markets.

Explain the number one problem you solve

Finally, write down the single biggest problem you help customers to solve. For example:

> 'We help businesses to make more money online'
> 'We help businesses to reclaim thousands of pounds through R&D tax credits'
> 'We help construction companies to avoid costly litigation caused by employer negligence'

Remember: this isn't about *how* you achieve those goals, but *why* people would be interested in working with you in the first place.

Put it all together

Once this is complete, all that's left to do is combine them into a short, meaningful sentence. For example:

> "Supplier Co. is a creative content provider, and we specialise in helping e-commerce sellers to maximise their sales revenue."

So long as you are talking to the right person in the correct type of business, this kind of statement should immediately strike a chord.

3. ESTABLISH YOUR CREDENTIALS

Now that the prospect knows what you do and why you do it, it's time to back that up with some evidence in the form of your case study – which needs to be short and sweet.

A 2016 study by Microsoft[4] found that the average person now has a shorter attention span than a goldfish.

Researchers in Canada surveyed 2,000 participants and studied the brain activity of 112 others using electroencephalograms (EEGs). The study found that since 2000, the average attention span has dropped from 12 seconds to 8 seconds: 1 second shorter than the oft-mocked goldfish.

These findings are powerful, but if those statistics are correct, you probably stopped listening halfway through that last paragraph. In which case, you'll just have to trust me: *brevity matters*. The last thing any Wonder Leads script needs is to be bogged down in detail, as it risks losing the prospect's attention and reduces the impact of the whole approach. Far better just to focus on the impact of the work and *why* it was carried out, rather than the actual execution or its specifics. The following four shortcuts will help you make your case study script nice and snappy.

Say who you helped

First, write down the name of the customer featuring in your case study (see Chapter 8, 'Preparing your story outline').

Say what they are

Next, write down a top-level description of that business and where they are based. For example, 'copywriter, Liverpool', or 'energy broker, New York'.

Say what you did

Then, write down the nature of the work you did for them, and when. For example:

'Magazine editing, January 2020'
'Renegotiation of energy supply contracts, October 2019'.

Say how you helped

Finally, write down the significant results that your work helped your customer to accomplish, and how long it took to achieve them. For example:

> 'Increased subscribers by 25 per cent within six months, leading to a 14 per cent increase in advertising revenue'
> 'A 34 per cent reduction in energy bills within 12 months'.

If the case study behind these statistics is complete, these facts and figures should be readily available. If not, this is a sign that the case study needs further work: it's advisable to go back to the customer at the centre of the case study and try to extract a few more salient details to strengthen the narrative.

If your work is fortunate enough to have resulted in multiple benefits, it's OK to list them all – just don't go too overboard! It's fine to stick to the headline grabbers: the statistics that any prospect would be most keen to replicate in their own business. Stuffing a script with too many benefits can reduce the overall impact of your communication: it waters down the most meaningful points.

Put it all together

Now it's time to build these into an impactful statement. For example:

> "To give you an example, last year we took over the content production for BigShop.com based in London. Within six months, their unique page views had risen by 37 per cent, leading to sales growth of 23 per cent. In the same period we also grew their subscriber base by 34 per cent, resulting in a 19 per cent upturn in advertising revenue."

As always, it pays to concentrate on using the least words possible to get the message across: it makes the story much easier to follow.

4. POINT THEM SOMEWHERE GREAT

Remember all that hard work you put into getting your case study into shape? Well, this is the point where it finally pays off, because now we're going to introduce it – we just need to be careful about how that happens. The more you try to push, the less likely they are to play ball.

> It's key to avoid making a prospect feel like they're being forced into action: it isn't just impolite, it's bad for business.
>
> A 2016 HubSpot survey on sales perception[5] found that 61 per cent of buyers would have a more pleasant sales experience if sellers were not pushy. That's a healthy majority of people who will be put off by an aggressive approach.

Instead, it's better to present the *option* of learning a bit more, if the prospect is so inclined. This is also the point where the layout of your landing page dictates the exact words you say. (We'll look at this in more detail in Chapter 14 on landing pages). For now, we can safely assume that the video your prospect is watching has a button underneath linking direct to your case study, so it's fine just to say something along the lines of:

> "If you want to find out more about the project, all you need to do is follow the link just below the video you are watching now."

This type of statement is friendly, helpful and makes it clear that any obligation to act on the part of the prospect is entirely in their control.

5. PLANT HELPFUL SEEDS

Now our prospect knows how our business has helped another customer, so we need to make them aware that it could help them too. This is the most delicate part of the script, as it's easy to switch into sales mode: reeling off lists of product information and add-on services, or directly asking for meetings to 'discuss things further'.

This is ill-advised. To explain why, it might be useful to revisit our earlier discussion on sales triggers (in Chapter 6, 'Identifying Prospects'). Sales triggers are markers that correspond to particular windows in time. During these windows, a business *may* be able to help a prospect solve a problem they are currently facing, but the chances of *actually* contacting a prospect in that window are incredibly slim. Your primary objective should be to leave a positive memory, so you are in a strong position as and when the next window arises. Openly acknowledging an awareness that it may not be the right time not only removes pushiness, but shows an understanding of the buyer's world – which in turn helps to build greater trust and confidence.

In the HubSpot Sales Perception survey mentioned previously, the only thing that buyers valued more than the seller not being pushy was their ability to listen to customer needs. A Wonder Leads video is just a one-way conversation, but showing empathy in the language used ensures that when that window does open, the conversation can start on the right foot.

Now we're ready to assemble all of this into a coherent statement. For example:

> "I know it's unlikely to be the right time for you now, but if you're looking for some additional assistance at some point down the line – perhaps to grow your audience, improve customer retention, or increase sales – it would be great to have a chat, because I think what we do can really help to achieve those types of goals."

It's worth paying attention to the way this statement ends.

First, it makes it clear that all that is being suggested is an informal conversation: no pressing for a sales meeting, product demonstration or any other detailed discussion. After all, until a proper two-way conversation has been held, neither of your companies will know if you might be a good fit for each other. Second, we aren't pushing our objectives onto them, simply reinforcing the point that our main interest is helping them achieve their own goals. This approach plays a vital role in establishing you as a person of considerable value.

6. LEAVE ON AN UPBEAT NOTE

Saying 'thanks' is the best way to conclude your video. Adding a personal touch to the ending by using the person's name again is highly recommended: not only does it build special rapport, but makes it even more evident to the prospect that the video has been created especially for them. Finally, it's always nice to end on a high note by sending your best wishes to your prospect and their team. For example:

> "In the meantime, thanks very much for listening, George. And I wish you and all the team at Prospect Co. a really great year."

That isn't just good manners – it's sound business sense. When one business succeeds, it creates opportunities for others to do the same – so be generous with your positive vibes. The world deserves it!

This handy checklist will help you put your script together

SCRIPT BUILDER

1. Lead with a greeting

- ❑ Begin by saying "Hello".
- ❑ Use the person's first name.
- ❑ Express gratitude for connecting.
- ❑ Apologise for taking their time.
- ❑ Make it clear you are not selling.
- ❑ Personalise your introduction whenever possible.

2. Provide some background

- ❑ Write a one to three-word description of your business.
- ❑ Write down which customer segments you best serve.
- ❑ Write down the single biggest problem you help those customers to solve.
- ❑ Formulate the elements above into a short and meaningful sentence.

3. Establish your credentials

- ❑ Reference a previous client where the impact of your work has been significant.
- ❑ Make sure they're relevant to as many connections as possible.
- ❑ Explain when you helped them.
- ❑ Explain what you did.
- ❑ Outline the results they achieved.
- ❑ Explain how long it took to see those results.

- ❑ Explain the primary benefit your customer experienced as a result.

4. Point them somewhere great

- ❑ Quickly explain how they can read more about it.
- ❑ Make sure they know that taking this step is entirely optional.

5. Plant helpful seeds

- ❑ Acknowledge that the timing is unlikely to be right for them now.
- ❑ Mention some of the pain triggers that may warrant a conversation with you.
- ❑ Explain that these are the problems you can help them overcome.
- ❑ Ask to have an informal conversation, should those problems ever arise.

6. Leave on an upbeat note

- ❑ Repeat their first name.
- ❑ Thank them for their time listening to your message.
- ❑ Send a positive message to them and their team.

Memorise your script

Reciting a script from memory is essential to delivering a Wonder Leads video. Reading a script out loud looks incredibly forced, more like auditioning for a job on a TV talent show than trying to engage another person in conversation.

Wonder Leads are personal introductions from you to your prospect. Unlike famous actors, TV presenters, politicians or public speakers, your target probably won't have a clue who you are. They might never have heard your voice, let alone watch your every move as you speak. Sadly, this means you're unlikely to have any social currency to cash in.

> Imagine you and I are meeting for the first time. You say "Hello" and offer a few pleasantries, but when my turn comes to speak, I pull out a piece of paper from my coat pocket and start reading you a response. At this point you're probably thinking I'm some strange kind of stalker who's been secretly planning this encounter for the past 20 years. Either that, or you're assuming I have so little confidence in my conversational abilities that I have to write down every potential reply in advance!
>
> Either way, it's unlikely you'll be responding to me as positively as you otherwise might.

By the end of the video, our goal is to make the prospect feel like they know us a little better, but it's a struggle if our attention is focused on a page of words rather than the quality of our delivery. Being natural in front of the camera means talking fluently and freely, with freedom to pause and riff on words whenever it feels right – just like a normal, introductory conversation. For that to happen, we need to know our script by heart.

Thankfully, we aren't talking about etching a novel into your hippocampus, as we've established that a Wonder Leads video is 2 minutes maximum. The average pop song is around 3 minutes long – so if you can sing along with just one popular music track, be it The Beatles, Ed Sheeran or Metallica, you'll easily memorise your Wonder Leads script.

For those who aren't naturally good at remembering things, help is at hand. The best place to start is the advice offered by the landmark 1917 study by Arthur Gates,[6] a professor of educational psychology at Columbia University.

Gates found that the quickest way to commit a passage to memory was to spend one-third of your time memorising the text, and the remaining two-thirds practising it. The act of learning in this way, with more time spent reciting, helps to forge the neural pathways that allow you to recall the information more efficiently at a later date.

To begin with, give yourself an hour. Start by reading your text thoroughly for 20 minutes, then spend the next 40 minutes trying to repeat as much of it as possible without looking. If you come unstuck, glance at it then try again – you'll be reciting it fluently before you know it. The more you repeat those practice sessions, the deeper the knowledge will become ingrained in your memory. It also becomes quicker to access. If you want to be able to remember your script in the long term, it's a good idea to keep practising and reciting it over a period of days and weeks.

If you're like me, you might find it easier to learn by listening rather than reading.

Try doing a voice recording of your script on a smartphone or dictaphone. In this way, you can listen back and try to pre-empt what is coming next.

I do this on my commute to work: it's a great way to turn travel time into learning time without having to speak or fiddle about with bits of paper. Once you can confidently reel off your script two or three times in a row without a mistake, you're ready to start recording.

Personalise whenever you can

Before we finish up this section on scriptwriting, let's look at one of the most significant improvements you can make to the scriptwriting process – indeed, to the entire Wonder Leads process: taking your script off-piste with a deeper level of personalisation.

Wonder Leads videos are exceptionally personal compared with almost any other form of business development. They require more effort to deliver, and if you follow the process, your prospects will appreciate that additional effort. The thing is, you'll probably be using the one script to deliver your videos, which means sending the same message to everyone for the most part.

Using the prospect's name and company is a critical start towards personalisation, but you can forge even stronger connections by taking it a step further.

Almost everyone responds better to more personalised content. A 2018 study by HubSpot analysed more than 330,000 call-to-action blocks on websites.[7] The research showed that personalised calls to action resulted in 202 per cent more conversions than non-personalised ones.

In another example, the UK tour operator Co-operative Travel saw a 95 per cent increase in visitors, and a 217 per cent increase in revenue, as a direct result of implementing personalisation on its website.[8]

Compared with a one-size-fits-all approach, it's clear that personalisation is better at driving action. But it's also important to mention that it would not be a good idea to create a completely unique script for each prospect you contact. While there's little doubt that the response results would be off-the-scale, writing a fully personalised script for every target would require a massive investment of time and energy, offering diminishing returns. It would be incredibly hard to send out enough introductions to maintain a steady flow of leads.

Instead, we are just talking about using a few relevant details to add an extra layer of depth to the messages you send. This personalisation gives you an opportunity to identify with your prospect and deliver a message that they will value more deeply.[9]

In practice, personalising an introduction video means doing a little bit of research immediately before recording. It's a great idea to have a laptop handy during your filming sessions, as this makes it easy to jump onto your prospect's LinkedIn profile (more on this in Chapter 11). Because the prospect is now part of your first-degree network, you have the privilege of being able to view their full profile and activity stream – all excellent sources of information.

Activity feeds allow you to see the topics currently occupying the prospect's mind, through their comments on posts and the news articles they've shared. Profile pages can be quite dull affairs, but they do provide nuggets of information which can be put to good use. Business wins, awards, charity initiatives, promotions, shared interests, speeches, event attendance and news articles all provide talking points that can be weaved into a script to make it more personal.

I once sent an introduction video to a group CEO of a large manufacturing business. Before recording I went through my usual routine, clicking on his profile page and looking at some of his most recent activity for inspiration. I couldn't see anything that immediately grabbed me, but then I noticed something he had written in his bio.

The prospect had shared his set of personal values. I'm a great believer in the importance of personal values, and many of the ones he listed were those I shared. There was one about remembering to bring a smile to your work that struck a particular chord.

When I recorded his video, I ad-libbed my standard script and mentioned how I shared the same ethos. I did this just after the initial introduction thanking him for connecting with me. In all it took just 2 minutes to find the information; it then took me another minute or so to work out what to say.

Once I had included this, the extra personalisation added around ten extra seconds to my typical video message duration.

I don't know if it was because of the extra personalisation, but I got a response within 5 minutes of his viewing the video. It wasn't a direct lead, but it was a positive 'thank you' – and it included a referral to another contact within his organisation.

That's a pretty decent result for less than 5 minutes of extra effort.

This was certainly not an isolated case. Analysis of my results shows that Wonder Leads videos with a personalised message like the one described earlier, result in significantly better outcomes across the board (Table 1).

Table 1: Impact of personalisation on viewed Wonder Leads videos

	Response rate	Positive comments	Average response speed to initial sharing message	Lead-generation rate
Personalised	100%	61%	0.2 days	39%
Standard	73%	23%	5.3 days	12.5%

From my own results, personalised introductions lead to 27 per cent higher response rates than videos using a standard script. They also generate 38 per cent more highly positive responses. Prospects also respond more quickly to personalised videos than standard ones: 26 times faster to be precise. This is likely because the value delivered in a personalised video is more noticeable, meaning the recipient's psychological need to acknowledge a personal gesture is more pressing. That is fundamentally what the Law of Reciprocity[10] is all about.

My evidence suggests that personalised videos also lead to faster responses at subsequent touchpoints. Replies to my insight shares following a personalised video have been three times faster than insight sent after a regular video.

This leads me to the inevitable conclusion that personalised video helps to build a stronger lasting connection – one that continues to pay dividends down the line.

Whatever your view on personalised content, there is no denying the statistical advantage it offers. To get even more out of the Wonder Leads process, try to look out for ways to personalise your videos. It'll certainly be time well spent.

ACTION POINTS

1. **Empathise.** Write every sentence from your prospect's perspective.
2. **Personalise.** Use your prospect's name, company and other relevant details to increase engagement in your message whenever possible.
3. **Don't overstay your welcome.** Keep your script as short as you can without losing the purpose.
4. **Focus on results.** Concentrate your message on the value you're capable of delivering, rather than the detail of how you deliver it.
5. **Memorise.** Use the one-third memorising, two-thirds practising technique to learn your script by heart, so you can deliver with fluency.
6. **Use the Wonder Leads Script Builder** to guide you through the essential elements for your script.

With your script finally wrapped up and all your content resources in place, it's time to check your teeth and comb that hair – because your moment in the spotlight awaits!

PART V

FILMING

109

10

Introduction to Filming

f you're anything like me, the initial thought of being filmed on-camera is a nailed-on nightmare scenario – probably up there with speaking to a room full of high-powered dignitaries, or being told you can't open your Christmas presents until after the Queen's speech.

It's entirely natural to be apprehensive about appearing on-camera. Most people aren't comfortable being in the limelight: alone, exposed, where every move is being recorded and captured for time immortal. Put it that way, it does sound terrifying. The important thing to note is that these apprehensions are, for the most part, complete fabrications by a part of the brain that's better suited to life in a cave than the 21st century.

In his bestselling book, *The Chimp Paradox*,[1] consultant psychiatrist Professor Steve Peters uses the analogy of a chimp to describe our instant, emotional reactions to different situations. Our inner chimp is quick-minded, rash and lacking in even the most basic forms of judgement: it tells you to stay away from danger, and run at the first sign of trouble. The reality is almost always less daunting than that inner chimp would have us believe.

The best way to conquer the fears imposed by our chimp is to programme our brain with better ways of dealing with situations: that way, it is overridden by logic and reason. When it comes to filming a Wonder Leads video, overcoming the chimp means good preparation and practise. The first step is to have the right equipment at hand.

Essential equipment

Your goal is to create a professional-looking digital video, so a few tools are key to make it happen. You might be lucky enough to have a lot of recording equipment available already – if so, great! It'll enable the filming process to be up and running more quickly. If you're starting from scratch, that's fine: we aren't looking to replicate a BBC studio inside your office. Everything on the following pages has been chosen to achieve the best results while keeping cost to a minimum. (You can thank my status as an adopted Yorkshireman for that.)

1. CHOOSE A DIGITAL CAMERA

The one piece of equipment you cannot manage without is a camera. "Perfect! I've got one on my smartphone." Well yes, but let me ask: what sort of impression do you want to make? As amazing inventions as smartphones are, they can't do everything well. They're awful for writing documents. Editing a spreadsheet on one is like eating glass. Designing something on one is artistic waterboarding (although having seen David Hockney's 'Spring' series of iPad paintings up-close recently, I may be shifting my view on that).

The thing is, no matter how hard someone tries to film themselves on a smartphone, the results are the same: the video ends up looking like something they would send their mum, and a Wonder Leads presentation needs to be better than that. The same goes for webcams.

Instead, I recommend using a digital SLR (DSLR) camera. They're a great option, because they:

- Are relatively cheap
- Can connect with a wide variety of devices
- Have a range of readily available accessories
- Usually support high-quality video filming

It doesn't matter what DSLR you buy. The most popular brands are Canon and Nikon, but there are many other established manufacturers offering great cameras, including Leica, Fuji and Sony, to name but a few. You can easily spend thousands on a camera from one of these manufacturers, but it isn't necessary: a top-level camera is definitely not required to create an introduction video. And it doesn't have to be new either: second-hand is just as fine.

Just be sure to check that the camera supports the following:

- HD video filming (we won't be shooting in HD, but this shows the camera is of a suitable standard)
- High-capacity standard definition (SD) cards
- External microphones
- Remote controls
- Direct download to a computer.

If the camera you're using or considering buying ticks these boxes, you are up, up and away.

Of course, it's equally fine to use a video camera instead of a DSLR. They can be picked up pretty cheaply, and certainly enable the process to get started. The main reason I prefer a DSLR is image quality and the ability to change the lens. Only the most expensive kinds of video cameras can interchange lenses, whereas you can fit a wide variety of different lenses to almost any DSLR. Switching the lens can make a massive difference to the final aesthetic of a video – something we'll be looking at in the next section ('Optional equipment').

> The camera I started out using – and still use now – is a ten-year-old Canon EOS 550D. It might be missing a few of the bells and whistles that modern cameras have, but it does everything I need, and the footage it captures is excellent.

2. USE A STURDY TRIPOD

A DSLR camera is quite heavy: there's no way you could hold it in your hand and film yourself for any length of time – and even if you were to, it would look terrible. Unless a plethora of colleagues are available with very little to do, it's highly unlikely that another person will be free to hold the camera for you and do the filming, so the next bit of kit on our shopping list is a tripod.

Again, the make and model are irrelevant: all that matters is that its maximum height extension can match – preferably exceed – your physical height, to ensure a suitable filming angle. Depending on the facilities available at your filming location, another option could be to use a smaller tripod or Gorillapod, which can be placed on a nearby surface.

While not essential, it is wise to consider your tripod's stability, as some of the cheaper ones can be flimsy and unstable, especially at their maximum extension. Also, some tripods might not be fully adjustable, which can make setting up a shot more of a pain.

The final thing to consider is whether your camera fits. Most tripods include a quick release base plate that screws into the bottom of the camera: this allows the camera to be put on and taken off quickly. If yours doesn't, spares or a replacement can be easily found online.

My current tripod cost less than £30, with a base plate. It has certainly done a job, but it is a little on the light side. I overcome this with the photographer's classic trick: hanging the camera bag off the middle of tripod to weigh it down. But it's my one piece of equipment up for replacement, as a more solid set-up in a busy office environment would be better.

3. STOCK UP ON HIGH-CAPACITY BATTERIES

Shooting video requires intensive battery usage, especially on older devices. Depending on how long your filming sessions intend to last, it's wise to prepare for one or more battery changes, and definitely to invest in some spares to avoid running out of power on the day.

Your camera might include one or two spare batteries – if so, that's good, but do check that they are the highest capacity the camera can support, as often a camera can take batteries with a much longer life than the ones supplied with it. It's worth searching online for a few options, just to see if anything better is available. This way you can record for longer without interruption – which all goes towards making your filming process smoother and more enjoyable.

The other item you'll need is a separate charger, to recharge spent batteries while you're still filming. Most new DSLRs come with a charger but this is something just to double-check, especially if you're buying second-hand.

> The high-capacity batteries I purchased hold three times more charge than the standard ones that came with my camera. They cost less than £15 for two.

4. GET HIGH-CAPACITY SD CARDS

Shooting video isn't just intensive on batteries, but on storage too. The SD memory cards that come as standard with most digital cameras are more suited to general photography than video: a card with high read-write speed is essential due to the large amount of data being captured and recorded at the same time. The card also needs high storage capacity, as a raw file for a video introduction can easily take up several hundred megabytes (a lot more, if shooting in HD). It won't take many reshoots before a standard 2GB SD card is being pushed.‡

Do invest in a new card (and be sure to get one or two extra as back-ups), and check that it's compatible with your make and model of camera.§

> The high read-write rate, 32GB SD card I use in my Canon cost less than £25 and can store around 3 hours of HD video: that's enough for more than 100 introductory videos in one go.

---

‡ This webpage is a handy guide to choosing the right size and type of card: 42 West (2016) 'Picking the right SD card: What do the numbers mean?', 19 December. Available at: www.adorama.com/alc/7809/article/picking-right-sd-card-what-do-numbers-mean

§ At websites such as mrmemory.co.uk you can type in the name of your camera, and it automatically shows you which cards match your device.

5. USE A LAPEL MICROPHONE

Any DSLR which can capture HD video features an in-built microphone. While this is fine for personal videos, when it comes to shooting something more professional, they rarely cut the mustard – so an external mic is recommended.

Unless you have access to a professional studio, the reality is that you will be filming your video in a relatively standard working environment. The average office space is sparsely decorated, with minimal soft furnishings and lots of hard surfaces – all of these create echo. The further you move from the mic (in an introduction video, it's likely to be several metres away from the camera), the more the sound reverberates. Echoes sound terrible on-camera: they make following your delivery hard, sometimes impossible.

You could spend thousands on soundproofing your office or buying a custom sound isolation booth, which undoubtedly would give you the best sound performance imaginable, but it isn't necessary. Perfectly good alternatives can handle this for a fraction of the cost.

A lapel (lavalier) mic is a small, clip-on device that attaches to your clothing at about chest level. They're most commonly seen on TV, especially in news broadcasts – they pick up the reporter's voice while eliminating noise from further away. A lapel mic works best when attached to a top or jacket, but it can be done discreetly: with the right camera angle, it's perfectly possible to hide it from view altogether by wearing it slightly lower than usual or even taping it directly to the chest underneath clothing, and with minimal loss of sound quality.

> I've tested a lot of different mics, and the lapel mic is the best quality, most convenient and cheapest solution I've come across. My personal favourite cost less than £20.

6. GET A GOOD-LENGTH EXTENSION LEAD

Because you're going to be filming your Wonder Leads video at a distance from the camera, it's unlikely that the cable supplied with your mic will be long enough to plug into the camera and reach you. A good-quality extension lead helps to comfortably bridge the distance between you and the camera, without pulling wires or veering visibly into shot.

A cable at least 3 metres long is suitable – ideally, 5 metres. That might be more than you need; but as every good roadie knows, it's better to have too much slack than not enough! Any excess length can be easily tidied up with a cable tie.

When buying an extension cable, be sure to check that it has the right jacks for both the mic and your camera. Sometimes, standard lapel mic cable jacks are only suitable for smartphone use: even though they look the same and may fit into the camera, they are different from what most DSLR cameras need to capture external audio.

The difference is the number of black rings on the connector: a smartphone uses a jack with three rings, whereas most DSLR cameras only have two rings. This is important, because if you don't have the right type of jack, it won't record the sound. With a bit of luck, your mic purchase will include a short cable to convert the smartphone-type connection to the DSLR-type (the one I bought did). If you do have the right converter, just make sure that the extension cable you are buying is the correct two-ring type, so that it plugs into your camera without any problems.

Another option is a wireless lapel mic, which eliminates extension leads altogether. Wireless mics are more expensive than the wired versions and need a separate power source, usually batteries. This presents another potential problem: running out of charge in the middle of filming.

I'm always looking for ways to avoid having to refilm anything, so for that reason I prefer the wired version. I use a 5-metre heavy-duty cable that I bought online for less than £10. The cable is braided, which makes it much less likely to get damaged or tangled.

7. USE A REMOTE SHUTTER BUTTON

As mentioned previously, the most likely scenario is that you are going to be filming yourself, alone, several metres away from the camera. Unless you've been blessed with the wingspan of a Wandering Albatross,[2] this presents a problem. A remote control starts and stops the filming function on a camera via a small, handheld button. Most modern remotes are wireless.

> The remote I use is a Canon-compatible wireless that works by infrared: it cost less than £5 online. All I have to do is set up the shot, put the camera into 'video' mode, point my remote at the camera and press a button.
>
> It's incredibly handy, because it means I can easily record individual videos for each person I'm contacting, rather than having to record and extract each video from one large file. Doing this also helps to preserve battery life. It's an essential piece of kit.

Optional equipment

The list of essential equipment we have considered above isn't definitive. If your budget can stretch a little further, you might want to consider the following extras to improve both your filming process and video quality.

1. TRY A 50MM PRIME LENS

Have you ever seen a portrait photo and instantly felt that it looks more dynamic and professional? Even if you know little about photography, you'll have noticed that these photos share the same characteristics: great lighting and *depth*. Much of this is dependent on the lens.

Most digital cameras come with an 18–55mm zoom lens as standard. All-rounders, they can tackle any kind of photography from portraits to landscapes, but they don't offer much out of the ordinary: the resulting image is likely to depend on the subject and setting, rather than the camera itself. To give your videos a more dynamic feel, consider investing in a 50mm f/1.8 lens for your DSLR. A fixed prime lens can focus on the foreground and blur out the background (known as 'bokeh') – it takes visuals to another level.

A 50mm prime lens also allows approximately five times the amount of light into a camera's sensor than a standard-issue lens, which significantly enhances the quality of a shot – even in a location with low natural light.

> I have a 50mm prime lens compatible with my Canon. It cost me around £50, and is hands down the best accessory in my kit bag. If your budget can stretch, it might pay to get one to experience the difference.

2. TAKE ADVANTAGE OF TETHERING SOFTWARE

Framing the picture correctly, and making sure you are in focus, are the most challenging parts of filming yourself. After all, your camera is pointing at you, and you can't see what it sees. Many new DSLRs have a mini flip-screen that allows the user to see what the camera is looking at, much like the front-facing camera on a smartphone.

This sounds ideal, but the reality is that the flip-screen is small. It's great if the camera is being used handheld, but as soon as you move any distance away, it becomes difficult to see any detail, including whether the camera is in focus.

Tethering software connects a camera with a computer and controls it via software: you can see what the camera sees, as if you are looking through the viewfinder (known as a 'slave' display). The software also enables control over other functions such as autofocus and remote triggering, which means a shot can be lined up perfectly from a marked location, and the correct focus achieved at the click of a button. All you need is an autofocus lens and a compatible extension cable, which should be long enough to bridge the gap between your camera and wherever your computer is placed.

Canon gives access to a tethering facility through its EOS Utility software, which can be downloaded for free from its website (only compatible with Canon DSLRs). At the time of writing, Nikon doesn't have an equivalent to EOS Utility, but there are plenty of free and paid software options that work with its cameras. Solutions are available for other DSLR brands too: just search for 'tethering software' with the name of the camera you own or are considering buying, to see what's available.

I usually put my computer on a table in front of where I'm standing to record my videos. Generally, I use a laptop as it's easy to move around, plus I can angle the screen to be able to see it from any position.

My camera remote also works with the tethering software, which means I can start and stop recordings without having to fiddle about with the computer keyboard, once everything is set up correctly.

3. EXPERIMENT WITH A GREEN SCREEN

If you have access to the right editing software and are technically proficient, a green screen might be the perfect way to take your videos to a whole new creative level.

A green screen enables the *chroma key compositing* technique: that is, filming in front of a green (or sometimes blue) cloth, then using post-production wizardry to isolate the subject from the green background and place them in a completely different scene.

Green screen techniques form the backbone of the computer-generated imagery (CGI) effects we've seen in the movies, especially action films. This might seem out of reach to the average person, but many software packages can do all the heavy lifting for you at the touch of a button. For example, iMovie (bundled for free with Apple desktops and laptops) and Filmora (less than $50 for a one-year licence) both include simple green-screen functionality. All you need is to shoot a video in front of a green screen, select a couple of green screen options, then insert a picture or second video clip behind the isolated footage. If you use the same background clip for every video, a green screen only adds a couple of extra clicks to the editing process (we'll be looking at this in Chapter 13). This process does require a little more software knowledge and time to create: it's only advisable for those who have the time and inclination to learn and experiment properly.

Still, the benefits of this technique are that you can free yourself from location constraints and put yourself anywhere you want to be: a corner office suite overlooking a river, in a relaxed roof garden, even on stage at the Royal Albert Hall! If you don't feel that daring, then solid colours, a rolling logo animation or a choice photo could work just as well. The only limit is your imagination.

> I don't use it often, but when I want to make a big bang for a particularly important prospect, I bring out my 1.5 x 2-metre foldable green screen, which I bought online for less than £30. It's easily stored, and works perfectly.

4. LIGHTING

The ideal scenario when shooting is to use natural light (more on this below, under 'Use natural light'). Lighting a room artificially is a real art. The light given off by most in-built ceiling lights can be harsh, creating unsympathetic shadows on the subject; the solution is to use directional lights.

Professional lighting equipment can be expensive, running into the thousands – but you don't need to spend a lot to improve the quality of artificial lighting. There are some great ways to improve your lighting with minimal investment. TechSmith (the software house behind Snaggit and Screencast) has an excellent article, 'How to Get the Perfect Lighting for Video',[3] which I heartily recommend if you need more guidance. It explores a range of options from budget to professional, including tips on how to achieve natural-feel lighting.

Use this handy checklist to ensure all the necessary kit is present and correct for your Wonder Leads video shoot.

EQUIPMENT CHECKLIST

Essential

- ☐ DSLR Camera (with HD video shooting capacity)
- ☐ Tripod
- ☐ Remote control
- ☐ Lapel microphone
- ☐ Spare high-capacity batteries
- ☐ High-capacity SD cards
- ☐ Extension leads

Optional

- ☐ 50mm f/1.8 fixed prime lens
- ☐ Laptop and tethering software
- ☐ Green screen
- ☐ Lighting kit

ACTION POINTS

1. **Spend wisely.** You don't need top of the range equipment. It's fine to start with items that do the job, then upgrade if necessary.
2. **Make use of technology.** Use tethering software on a nearby computer to overcome the challenges of filming on your own.

3. **Try things out.** Test your equipment to make sure everything is compatible and functions well in your shooting environment.
4. **Use the Wonder Leads Equipment Checklist** to ensure all your kit is in place before filming.

Location

Location, location, location. It matters in property, and it matters when creating great Wonder Leads videos. Your chosen place for filming could make all the difference to the success of your videos, so let's look at the top four requirements for a perfect set.

1. CHOOSE SOMEWHERE QUIET

The goal is to ensure your prospect concentrates on what you're saying, rather than what is going on around you, so it's key to choose a location that's as quiet as possible. A factory floor, for example, is unlikely to be suitable; neither is a call centre. Not only will the sound be distracting to you while recording, but random interjections and high levels of background noise can make listening to a video very difficult.

Instead, pick somewhere sufficiently distant from the action. If that isn't possible, then film at a time when all the hubbub has died away, such as early morning or late at night.

2. KEEP OTHER PEOPLE AWAY

If you are anything like me, then interruptions at work arrive ten to the dozen, whether it's phones ringing, emails pinging or colleagues singing. Interruptions are the arch-enemy of recording: it's the reason for the big red 'STOP' lights outside music rehearsal rooms, and the 'ON AIR' signs frightening would-be interjectors away from live TV studios.

Be sure to commandeer a location specifically for your purposes, and bar other people from it, if necessary – at least for one or two hours at a time.

....

3. USE NATURAL LIGHT

It's impossible to underestimate the importance of good, natural lighting while filming: it makes everything look better, especially you. This can be a challenge in some working environments, particularly if the preferred location is in the centre of a large building. Still, even the smallest amount of natural light can make all the difference, especially when combined with the right camera lens.

If you are lucky enough to have good natural light and a prime lens, try switching off the lights in the room: it might seem dark at first, but that's usually because our eyes have become accustomed to artificial lighting. It is amazing how good images often come out on-camera in low natural light: a million miles better than artificial lighting.

Obviously, this only applies in daylight hours. If shooting is happening at night or in a location with poor natural light, you will need to use artificial light.

....

4. BACKGROUNDS

——————

1. Good backgrounds

If you have an enviable office space, this is your opportunity to use it to your advantage. A great shot of your premises, whether it showcases the quality of interior design or striking architecture, can form the perfect backdrop to a Wonder Leads video.

If your premises are a bit bland (and let's face it, most offices are), then it might be worth sprucing them up a bit, otherwise it risks undermining the quality of the video. This doesn't have to mean hiring Lawrence Llewellyn-Bowen to redecorate your boardroom (although no doubt you'd have a marvellous talking point, if you did!). The look of a place can be quickly improved by putting some great artwork on the walls, using vinyl graphics to customise a wall with company branding, or employing a few choice items of furniture to bring it to life (Figure 2).

Modern interior   Good architecture

Figure 2: Good typical backgrounds

---

2. Bad backgrounds

Try to avoid shooting a video in a large room full of empty desks, as this can give the impression that a business lacks life. It would be better to have a few people working away quietly in the background than none at all. While it is important that the location has some visual interest, be careful that it isn't too busy. A location with lots of movement in the background or too much clutter on display can easily distract the prospect's attention away from the speaker. The background should subtly complement the introduction, not compete with it (Figure 3).

Too lifeless   Too boring

Figure 3: Bad typical backgrounds

ACTION POINTS

~~~~~

1. **Choose somewhere practical.** The ideal location will be quiet, private, sufficiently large for all your gear and somewhere you can access whenever you need it.

2. **Try to use natural light.** Natural lighting creates a superior look for your videos, so use it whenever practical. Consider a lighting kit if this isn't an option.

3. **Don't detract from your message.** Poor lighting and overly complex backgrounds may cause your prospect to lose focus on what you are saying.

4. **Make it feel welcoming.** Your location should be a positive reflection of your business – somewhere you feel proud to associate with your work.

5. **Add some personality.** Adding pictures, soft furnishings or subtle branding to a space can dramatically improve its overall look, and your confidence with it.

11

Preparation

To run the Wonder Leads framework efficiently means preparation. Without it, there's a real risk of wasting time redoing things for no good reason. (Believe me, I've been there. I've got the T-shirt. It is not one you want to wear!) The tips in this chapter might seem obvious, but they are key to the process and only take a few seconds.

If you don't want to end up throwing your camera out of a fifth-floor window for wasting hours filming, because you went to the loo and forgot to plug your microphone extension cable back in, here are the essential things to do before setting that camera rolling.

Take the basic preparatory steps

BLOCK OUT YOUR TIME

It's a good idea to run filming sessions in batches, because it takes a while to set up the recording space and download videos. Running videos in groups helps to benefit from economy of scale: a maximum of 20 videos is suitable for any single session; after that, enthusiasm tends to drift. Every Wonder Leads video you create needs to look and sound fresh, so anywhere between five and ten videos per session is a good target to aim for; it will be much easier to do more as you become familiar with the process.

In terms of planning time, it's fine to allow around 5 minutes or so to set up. If you are using a location for the first time, this is likely to take longer. Once you know where everything needs to go, it should be a 2-minute job. If your edited videos are roughly 1 minute 30 seconds long, with a bit of a pause at the beginning and the end, shooting ten videos will take somewhere in the region of 20 minutes to film. Do factor in preparation time to set up for the next video as well: as a rough guide, a couple of minutes in-between each one – so for the overall shoot, it's a good idea to allow around another 20 minutes.

Finally, also factor in extra time for retakes: that will be down to your skills in front of the camera. The more videos you shoot, the more proficient you will become, so retakes will be less likely. When starting out, do give yourself plenty of time for these: allow at least an hour. This means that your first ten videos are likely to take a good 2 hours in total to film. With practice, 5 or 10 minutes are probably all you'll need for retakes.

> I spent the best part of a day trying to film my first five videos, but by the end of the following week, I had recorded 15 in under an hour. It really does get quicker, the more you do it.

SET UP YOUR ENVIRONMENT

If you can, lock the door to your location and put up a 'Do Not Disturb: Filming in Progress' sign outside, which hopefully should stop others from accidentally interrupting the session.

It's also a good idea to check beforehand that no one is going to be doing any loud work nearby. There's nothing more frustrating than setting up to film, only for power drills to fire up in an adjoining room! Not only will the noise distract you, but it can be picked up on any kind of entry-level mic. It will definitely distract your prospect during play-back, making your video look amateurish. For the same reason, be sure to close any windows to block out as much external noise as possible.

Assuming it's daytime, the final check is for lighting. If you're shooting with natural light, open all the blinds and switch off the main overhead lighting. If artificial light is required, just be sure to check everything is powered on and set correctly.

CHECK YOUR PERSONAL APPEARANCE

Now the location is adequately prepared, you need to spend a couple of minutes getting yourself spruced-up: the part that many of us fear the most. A 2016 research study in the *Body Image* journal[1] found that only 28 per cent of men and 26 per cent of women are 'extremely satisfied' with their appearance. Nearly everyone has hang-ups because of the way they look. (For me, it's my trophy-like ears that led my teammates to nickname me 'Lugsy' while playing university football.)

The thing is, all we are comparing ourselves against is the idealistic, heavily-Photoshopped versions of people that we see splashed over the media. No one needs to look or act like Brad Pitt or Emma Stone to create a great Wonder Leads video; simply to present the very best version of ourselves now. Whatever reservations you might have about thinning hair, nose size or tooth whiteness, no one's going to notice. Your prospects are going to be far more focused on the words coming out of your mouth.

When it comes to checking appearance, simply concentrate on achieving a suitably professional look. I say *suitably*, because what you choose to wear very much depends on your unique circumstances. For those working in a corporate environment, targeting other corporate prospects, a suit is likely to be the way to go. By contrast, more relaxed attire may be appropriate for anyone targeting hip, young millennials for whom a suit is only for weddings and funerals. All that matters is feeling comfortable.

That said, there is compelling research indicating that clothing choice can make a significant difference, not only in how we perceive ourselves, but those around us.

In 2014, Dr Michael Kraus, Assistant Professor of Organisational Behaviour at Yale University, released a research paper on clothing and its effects on behaviour.[2]

In the study, Dr Kraus and colleagues examined the behaviour of 128 men in a role-playing exercise, where they had to bargain for a fair sale price of a valuable asset with another participant they had never met.

The men, from a broad range of social backgrounds, were divided into two halves, 'Targets' and 'Perceivers'. The Targets were assigned one of three experimental conditions: 'neutral (which included all Perceivers)', 'high-status' and 'low-status'. Their designated state had nothing to do with their actual social status. The neutral group were allowed to complete the exercise wearing their regular clothes, while the high-status group were asked to change into a business suit, shirt and dress shoes. The low-status group were told to wear a white T-shirt, joggers and plastic sandals.

Once dressed, the participants entered a second room, where they met their partner (the neutral Perceiver) for the first time. The two participants then engaged in a competitive negotiation in which they acted as chief financial officers of rival companies tasked with coming to a consensus on the sale price of a valuable asset.

The outcome of the study found that high-status participants were nearly twice as successful as their neutrally dressed rivals in the amount of profit they negotiated. Compared with their competitors wearing joggers, the results were even more stark, with high-status targets generating nearly three times as much profit as their low-status rivals.

Those are enormous differences. The study traced some of the results back to differences at the hormonal level, with participants wearing joggers experiencing a 20 per cent drop in testosterone levels from their pre-test level. There was no discernible drop in people wearing their regular clothes or suits.

This study was a one-to-one negotiating scenario, while Wonder Leads videos are one-way conversations. Still, it's a clear indication that outfit choice could well make a big difference – not only to your mindset, but the way you are perceived by the prospect.

Double-check your equipment

Checking every bit of equipment is essential, as one incorrect setting or a single loose lead can result in hours of lost filming time. The following section will guide you through the things you need to check before running a recording session.

1. CAMERA SET-UP

What follows are general checks for all types of camera. You should also consult manufacturer instructions for specific steps relating to your unique make and model.

Check the battery

Start by turning on the camera and checking the battery level. If it's low, replace the battery with a fresh one and put the other on charge.

Check SD card storage

If there are lots of old videos on the card which have already been downloaded, delete them. It's generally good practice to remove all the videos on a SD card after downloading a batch to a computer, as it prevents problems with running out of space while filming. It also makes it easier to know which files are current.

Select 540px video filming mode

After that, set your camera to video recording mode. It should support multiple video sizes during recording: the default is usually HD, perhaps even 4K – avoid these settings, as they're far too big and unnecessary for our purposes here. Your prospects are going to view your video on a mobile phone, tablet or desktop computer, rather than a 60-inch LED screen. HD and 4K recordings eat up masses of space on camera cards and computer hard drives, and take much longer to download.

If the camera supports it, film at 540px: it's perfectly fine for Wonder Leads purposes. If that option isn't available, it's fine to select the closest size up. It's inadvisable to go any smaller, as this can affect playback quality on devices with larger screens.

....

2. SHOT SET-UP

Now it's time to mount the camera on the tripod and check the framing. As we've identified, the simple way to get around this is to use a laptop with suitable tethering software (see Chapter 10). If that isn't an option, it's best to draft a colleague in for help, at least during the initial set-up.

Find the filming position

The first step is establishing the marks: the points between you and the tripod. It might take a bit of experimenting to find the right ones: your colleague may need to move the tripod and adjust its height and angle until the composition works. Be sure to set your camera to landscape format, *not* portrait: the video needs to be optimised for desktop computers and laptops, which display best in landscape.

Check that your upper body is clearly in view: ideally, in a central position, with a gap approximate to half head height between yourself and the top of the picture. If your head is too close to the top of the image, it will look strange, a bit like being crushed in a giant vice. The entire body doesn't have to be visible: if it is, it makes it difficult for the prospect to appreciate your facial expressions (an essential part of face-to-face communication, and one of the reasons that Wonder Leads can be so effective), so be sure to step closer to the camera.

Conversely, if you get too close, people might struggle to see your hands. Hand gestures play another big part in the way that humans read communication signals through body language, so they need to be in the picture at all times (see Chapter 12, 'Body language').

With all this in mind, depending on your location and the camera lens, 3–5 metres away is a reasonable distance to set the marks, simply adjust as your equipment and space dictate.

Physically mark positions

It's a good idea to physically mark the floor, so you can easily return to the same spots in future. Try to avoid using anything that could be knocked over or blown away: a couple of strips of duct or insulation tape placed just in front of your feet and at the outside edges of the tripod feet are ideal, making repositioning easy and quick enough to remove if necessary. (If you're filming in your office, be sure to tell the office cleaners, so they don't mistake them for rubbish!)

Check the focal position

Assuming the shot is fine and in focus, mark the focal position on the camera lens with a pencil. Around the edge of the lens, you will see several marks and numbers, and a longer central line. These indicate the current focal depth of the lens: this changes as the lens is twisted, which brings different elements of the picture into focus. It's easy for the focal point to change if the lens gets knocked accidentally. The focal point will also change whenever the shutter is depressed with autofocus enabled.

If you do that, the camera will start to focus on whatever is central in the picture at that time, so when you retake your mark, you'll no longer be in focus. It can be quite hard to spot if you are out of focus, especially if shooting solo without tethering software – and you really don't want to discover that after completing a big filming session: it means a potentially large number of retakes. Having a pencil mark to line up with makes it quick and easy to see if the lens is at the right position to start shooting. If you are using this technique, turn off autofocus on your lens once you've established the right focal point, otherwise it could kick in before the camera starts recording, homing in on something it shouldn't.

Microphone set-up

Next, it's time to plug in the mic. Attach the jack to the camera using the appropriate leads, and the mic to your clothing: ideally, about a foot away from your mouth. If you're wearing a jacket, blazer or cardigan, clipping it to your lapel is perfect. If not, it can be discreetly positioned – just be careful not to obstruct it in any way.

As mentioned previously, a mic can be hidden entirely from shot by wearing it lower down the body or attaching directly to the chest, but this can result in deterioration in sound quality: voice echo and unwanted noises, such as clothing rustles or rubbing hands.

> I once recorded ten videos with a mic placed low down, just out of shot. Only after I had filmed, downloaded and begun editing them did I realise they sounded like I was striking Thor's hammer every time I put my hands together.
>
> I had to shoot them all over again. If you can, try to keep your mic at middle-of-the-chest level – it will save you an awful lot of trouble!

Do a trial run

Now everything is set up, it is time to do a quick test. First, stand at your mark and start the camera recording, using the remote control. Wave at the camera (this is important, as we will see in Chapter 12), then begin speaking and moving your arms about for about 5 seconds or so. Then, stop the recording, go back to the camera and replay it to make sure everything looks and sounds as it should.

Here are a few common issues to look out for.

Does it have sound?

If there is no sound, there's probably an issue either with the mic or the leads connecting the mic to the camera. Check that the jacks are the right ones for your equipment and plugged in.

Is the sound clear?

If it sounds tinny, it might be recording through the in-built camera mic instead of the external mic. Check that the mic is plugged into the camera correctly. If the recording sounds muffled, check that the mic isn't rubbing on any clothing: if so, adjust its position so it's clear of interference.

Are you in focus?

Zoom in on the camera preview image to make sure your head is in focus. If not, check that the lens marker is in the right position. If that's OK, check that the tripod is on the correct mark and you were standing in the right spot.

If none of those are the problem, it's possible the marks have moved, or the tripod has changed position. You'll probably need to ask a colleague for help to reset the shot.

Are you correctly positioned in the picture?

Are you central in the shot, with face and arms clearly in view? Can you see your wave clearly without it being cut off? If the answer to any of these is no, you'll need to enlist a colleague's help or use your tethering software to reframe the picture.

Is the lighting correct?

If the picture looks too dark, you may need to adjust the ISO setting on the camera, which helps to control image brightness: the higher the ISO, the brighter the picture, so try experimenting with different settings to see if that helps.

The same goes if the picture is too bright and washed out. If the ISO has been adjusted and the image is still too dark, it might be time to switch on some overhead lighting. If strange shadows appear on your face or body, try turning some lights on and others off.

If that still isn't working, consider a lighting kit (see Chapter 10, 'Optional equipment').

How do you look?

Is there anything unusual about your appearance, do your clothes look unkempt, is there anything unwanted in your teeth or hair? If so, find a mirror and indulge in a spot of personal grooming. If a mirror isn't available, the front-facing camera on a smartphone will do the trick.

This handy checklist will help you cover all bases before you hit 'record'.

PRE-FILMING CHECKLIST

Environment

- ❑ Block out 5 minutes per video for filming, plus 5 minutes for set-up
- ❑ Mute all landlines and mobile phones in the room
- ❑ Make sure the scene is tidy
- ❑ Close all doors and windows to block out noise
- ❑ Allow as much natural light into the room as possible
- ❑ Put a 'Do Not Disturb' sign on the location door

Personal

- ❑ Check your personal appearance
- ❑ Run a final check of the script and any important facts
- ❑ Have your connections LinkedIn profile visible off-camera
- ❑ Double-check the pronunciation of your connection's name

Equipment

- ❑ Set up tripod and attach camera
- ❑ Ensure tripod is set to correct height and angle
- ❑ Attach mic to camera
- ❑ Attach mic to yourself (discreetly but unobstructed)
- ❑ Check camera is in 'video' mode and set to 540px
- ❑ Check camera focus
- ❑ Check camera lighting level
- ❑ Check camera battery level (and charge spare)
- ❑ Check remote control is operational

Testing

- ❑ Record a test movie (under 5 seconds is fine)
- ❑ Check the recording: does it sound OK?
- ❑ Are you correctly in focus?
- ❑ Does the lighting look OK?

Final touches

With all of our checks made, there are just a couple of final steps to help ensure our filming session runs as smoothly as possible.

1. KEEP THE SCRIPT HANDY

By this point, you will have memorised your script (see Chapter 9), but everyone can experience occasional brain fade. Print out a copy of the script as large as possible on a single sheet of A4 paper (if you'd rather avoid printing, a tablet computer is just as fine). Keeping your script to hand means you can refresh your memory easily, without losing time.

2. GET YOUR LIST OF CONTACTS READY

The final thing you need to do before filming starts is to draw up your shooting list. The simplest way to do this is to have a laptop nearby with your LinkedIn 'Connections' page open (under the 'My Network' tab). The first people you contact will be the most recent connections who haven't yet received an introduction from you.

Syncing your video intros with the order of connections is a great way to keep the Wonder Leads process neat and tidy: you'll know the next person to be contacted, and can check a prospect's details at-a-glance if you need to remind yourself of their name or company, should a mid-take brain-freeze occur.

ACTION POINTS

~~~~~

1. **Good preparation saves time.** A few minutes well spent checking things before the shoot can save you hours later.
2. **Don't assume everything's fine.** Always perform a quick test to make sure everything looks and sounds the way it should. Address any problems before starting a full session, to avoid reshoots.
3. **Choose the right outfit.** Wearing the right clothes can improve your confidence and the way you are perceived. Experiment with the outfits that work for you, and consider always keeping a spare set on hand at your location.
4. **Have the right information available.** Make sure your list of contacts and script are within easy reach, should you need them.
5. **Use the Wonder Leads Pre-filming Checklist** to help you cover all the bases before commencing a shoot.

12

Being On-camera

uality of delivery goes a long way to determining the success of a Wonder Leads video, but it doesn't require booking classes at your local amateur dramatics society. To be clear, while there is an element of performance about being on-camera, we are not talking about *acting*. Acting is for the likes of Tom Hanks and Whoopi Goldberg: they inhabit characters and bring them to life through the mediums of film and TV. The delivery for Wonder Leads videos has nothing to do with playing a role: all you need to do is be *you.*

That said, it's important to make sure it is the right type of you. (If anyone has ever found themselves rudely awoken by the neighbours at 4am for the third weekend on the trot, they'll know that there are some versions of themselves that won't look so hot on-camera!)

With this in mind, let's walk through some best practice to ensure your brief moment in the spotlight reflects the best version of you.

Dealing with nerves

There is one overriding feeling that most people following the Wonder Leads process for the first time might be experiencing now: *nerves.* Nerves about personal appearance or remembering details, being seen and correct pronunciation, or speaking too fast or slow. Above all, whether it's worth this considerable discomfort.

All of these feelings are totally natural. Nervousness and excitement are aroused emotions: in both states the heart beats faster, cortisol levels rise and the body prepares itself for action; but the difference between the two is that excitement is a positive emotion. When someone is excited, their brain conjures up images of all the things that could go well; when they're nervous, their mind fixates on all the things that could go badly.

As these two mindsets are almost identical in the way they alter our physical state, the trick is to alter our *perception* of that physical state to our advantage, and reframe it as *excitement*. It might feel that attempting to calm down would be a better approach, but as it turns out, it rarely has the desired effect.

In 2014, Alison Wood Brooks of Harvard Business School published a study into the effect of performance anxiety in the *Journal of Experimental Psychology*.[1] The study involved a series of experiments designed to test the possibility of reappraising anxiety as excitement.

First, the study surveyed respondents for the best advice to give someone anxious about a presentation, to establish the general wisdom on coping with performance anxiety. Of the respondents, 85 per cent said that the best way to deal with performance anxiety is to try and calm down.

Next, a separate group of 113 participants were asked to sing on a karaoke video game. Before the singing task, the organisers split the participants into three groups: the first group was told to say to themselves, 'I am anxious', the second, 'I am excited', while the third was asked to do nothing. The video game then measured how well they performed. Other experiments checked variables such as familiarity with the song and confidence in their singing.

In a similar experiment, the participants were asked to write and read a 2–3-minute public speech in front of one of the researchers. They were also told that the address was going to be recorded on video and judged later by a committee of peers. Before making their speech, the participants were randomly assigned to tell themselves either 'I am calm', or 'I am excited'. Three independent judges rated how well they delivered their speeches.

The results of the study were stark. The participants in the 'I am excited' group during the singing test displayed an average accuracy score of 80 per cent, compared with just 53 per cent in the 'I am anxious' group. The no self-assessment group scored 69 per cent accuracy, indicating that telling yourself 'I am excited' can improve performance, even if not feeling nervous beforehand.

In the speech experiment, the participants in the 'I am excited' group outscored those in the 'I am calm' group on every judging criterion, including persuasiveness, competence, confidence and persistence. They were also able to speak for nearly 30 per cent longer.

Few people consider themselves naturally comfortable on-camera, but many of the things we experience in life can be improved by handling them better internally. If you've followed the process so far, you should have an excellent script, firmly committed to memory, in a location that feels comfortable, wearing clothes that inspire confidence.

You are just moments away from recording a short video which could turn around the fortunes of your business. You have *every right* to feel excited!

Speaking

Quality of speech plays an essential part in how well a video introduction is received. Before you start channelling your inner Dr Martin Luther King, it's worth revisiting the reason for recording this video. It's being sent as a personal introduction – a friendly one at that. If you were to meet someone and they intoned like a Shakespearean actor, you'd raise an eyebrow or two. As we've identified previously, it's more useful to be yourself than to adopt a voice or persona which doesn't come naturally, but we can do some things to improve our speech.

In an article on Entrepreneur.com, author and business etiquette expert Jacqueline Whitmore shares some of her top tips for making your voice more effective.[2]

1. AVOID RUSHING

When we're nervous or excited, the physical changes in our body may well cause us to speak too fast, which can make us appear jittery and lacking in confidence. It may even cause a prospect to entirely lose the thread of what is being said.

While our Wonder Leads video needs to be brief, it should never be rushed. Try to speak at a comfortable pace that's easy to follow, pronouncing all of the syllables clearly. If it runs on too long, edit the script: never speed up your rate of speaking to compensate for excess words, because people may switch off.[3]

2. USE AN APPROPRIATE VOLUME

Finding the right sound level should be straightforward, because your speech is directed towards one person via a mic designed to pick up a natural speaking voice.

If your voice is naturally quiet, just check whether you're projecting enough to be picked up by your mic. For those with louder voices, check for the opposite: that the sound isn't distorted. If either of these happen, simply adjust your speaking volume.

3. DON'T HIDE YOUR ACCENT

Don't worry about accents: they all go to creating the wonderfully unique people we are. However, do make sure that what you say can be clearly understood, especially if you're contacting someone outside of your geographical area who might be unfamiliar with your dialect. If you have any concerns about this, just ask a friend or colleague for an impartial opinion.

4. ADJUST PITCH

Pitch describes the highness and lowness of a voice as it speaks: it gives people their distinguishable sound and provides vocal variety that makes listening more enjoyable. For example, higher notes are useful when asking questions, while lower notes can emphasise statements.[4] The best way to understand and improve pitch is to rehearse before going on-camera. Try reading your script into a voice recorder, then listening it back for critique. The ideal voice strikes a balance between professional and friendly.

5. CHANGE TEMPO

To make it pleasant for a prospect to follow, your general rhythm of speech should be smooth and confident. You can change tempo to alter the dynamics of your language in much the same way that changes in pace affect the way we interpret music. For example, slowing down can place greater emphasis on a word or passage, while speeding up can inject more excitement and energy. Just make sure that changes of pace are appropriate, otherwise it runs the risk of prospects disconnecting with the delivery.

6. USE PAUSES

While your natural inclination might be to keep speaking until you've finished the script, it's perfectly fine to stop and pause during delivery; it might actively help to take a second or two to draw breath midway through.

Public speaking tips from one of the world's most sought-after public speakers, Simon Sinek, include the use of deliberate pauses as a way to build anticipation and strengthen engagement.[5] When a prospect clicks play on your Wonder Leads introduction, they will be a captive audience for the next 2 minutes, so don't be afraid to pause if it's appropriate. It might prove to be the silent bridge that builds an even more powerful connection.

Body language

While on-camera, the most important thing to be aware of after speech is body language. As one of the principal ways in which humans communicate with each other, it's firmly embedded in our evolutionary past, pre-dating speech to a time when the majority of communication was similar to that of other animals: understanding and sending non-verbal cues.

Politicians are brilliant for studying body language. If you've ever watched one deliver a speech, live or on-camera, you're likely to have noticed there are particular ways they use their bodies to help them communicate. For one thing, they rarely point – at least not in the way that you, I or any average human would. Instead, they use their knuckles, or sometimes soften the gesture by cajoling a thumb in coordination with a crooked (no pun intended) index finger; this is because they receive copious media training, and know that finger-pointing can come across as aggressive and accusatory. Which doesn't usually go down well with the electorate.

Politicians rarely look down either: bowing the head forward, with eyes fixed on the floor, conveys defeat, shame or lying. If politicians weren't able to master their natural body language, we'd rarely get to see their faces at all. We'd probably just know them from whose hair is thinning the quickest.

Body language is a vast subject, beyond the scope of this book. For those interested in learning more, there are plenty of excellent books, such as *The Power of Body Language* by Joe Navarro,[6] or *Gravitas* by Caroline Goyder.[7] In the meantime, let's look at some of the most important considerations for your Wonder Leads recording.

....

1. ADOPT GOOD POSTURE

Always deliver your video from a standing position. Standing offers more authority than being seated, plus your prospect can read your body language more clearly. It has other benefits too, such as making your breathing more comfortable and improving voice projection.

In their publication 'Gestures: Your body speaks – how to become skilled in nonverbal communication',[8] Toastmasters, an international non-profit that educates people in the art of public speaking, recommends the following steps to help you get into a suitable pose for presenting:

1. First, stand up straight with your feet shoulder-width apart. Move one foot slightly ahead of the other, balancing your weight on the balls of your feet.
2. Next, relax your knees until they are straight, but not locked. Lean forward slightly, keeping your chest up and stomach in, and let your arms hang naturally by your sides with your fingers slightly curled.
3. Finally, raise your chin slightly. Once you are in position, take a few deep breaths and ask yourself if you feel comfortable. If you don't, shuffle your feet slightly until you do.

2. CONTROL MANNERISMS

I have a strange, unconscious tendency to touch my neck and chin when I'm feeling tense. It leaves me with a red mark on my neck, which looks like I've been desperately trying to remove a thread of dental floss from my beard.

While there are worse things I could be doing, it is quite distracting for anyone who notices it. It's also evident to anyone who does that I'm not relaxed.

This and other physical movements are precisely the kind of distractions to avoid. They make the speaker seem less confident, and take attention away from what's being communicated.

The best way to find out if you do this is to ask close friends and colleagues for an honest appraisal. It's also a good idea to record a whole video and review it to see if you might be doing anything odd: especially repeat actions such as rocking, swaying, licking lips, frowning, adjusting clothing, or turning the head or eyes from side-to-side – these all need to be removed whenever possible.

Unfortunately, concentrating on mannerisms can cause you to lose focus during filming, which is another reason why it's essential to memorise the script. The more calm, composed and natural you appear, the better the impression for your prospect.

....

3. USE POSITIVE GESTURES

Unlike mannerisms, gestures are intentional movements of the body that help to reinforce and add colour to your words. As a rule of thumb, try to keep hand and body gestures affirmative. Use them to reinforce the good things you have to say.

When it comes to gestures there is a lot to think about, but from a Wonder Leads perspective, we only need to consider two things.

Use natural hand gestures

If your natural gesturing style is quite exuberant, perhaps try to limit them a little, as too many can make a speaker look frantic on-camera. Also, be careful of using anything too dramatic, such as punching fists or moving around too quickly, as this can look unwantedly aggressive.

Start and end with a wave

Assuming it is culturally acceptable to do so, always start and end your video with a wave. It might feel a bit forced in the beginning, but there is an excellent reason for doing so. The waving gesture most often used in western cultures originates from the 18th century: it started as a form of salute, where enemy soldiers could show they carried no weapons and came in peace. Just like our historic soldiers, a Wonder Leads prospect needs to know straight from the off that we are *friendly*.

Waving within western cultures is what social scientists might describe as an 'emblem' or 'quotable gesture': they don't require speech to be understood. Not only that, but they are often understood cross-culturally too which makes them incredibly powerful.

Using a wave right at the start of a video makes it clear that the sender wants to say "Hello", which reduces any apprehension the viewer might have about its purpose or content. Similarly, waving at the end is a clear signal of leaving in peace, ending on an upbeat note.

If our video is being sent to someone from another culture, we need to be aware of whether such a gesture could be misinterpreted. For example, in Nigeria, waving the hand with the palm facing towards someone's face is considered highly offensive; the same is true in Greece.

If you are sending videos internationally, be sure to research cultural differences beforehand: find an alternative, quotable gesture which can be equally understood by your prospect without rubbing them up the wrong way.

4. FACIAL EXPRESSIONS

When we speak, our face communicates thoughts and feelings more than any other part of the body. It acts as the viewer's barometer, helping them understand what's going on inside the speaker. It tells them if you are happy or sad, comfortable or nervous – and can even lead them to trust or doubt your sincerity.[9]

Here are a few tips to help you shine.

Smile with your eyes

Because Wonder Leads videos are unashamedly positive, we want people to think we're a happy sort – a genuine smile can go a long way to achieve that goal. If you've ever been through the tortuous process that is an office photo shoot, you'll know that pulling off a winning, natural smile on-camera is not as simple as it might appear.

While your mouth is important, it's only one part of a winning smile: a pro trick is to smile with the eyes. Eyes play a big part in reinforcing the nature of a smile – if they don't compliment the mouth's expression, we can appear insincere.[10] Expressing your smile via both will help you avoid that.

_____

A little emotion goes a long way

In general, it's perfectly fine to express emotion when delivering a presentation. Used at an appropriate time, facial expressions add colour, variety and interest to a performance, and make it easier for a prospect to warm to the sender.

Staying relaxed and allowing our face to show natural changes also helps to avoid the dreaded 'death stare'. There's nothing worse than someone fixing their gaze at a camera for an entire recording, like a frightened rabbit: no expression or blinking, barely any breathing – a definite sign that the presenter is in deep discomfort.

If you appear uncomfortable, that will almost certainly make your prospect uncomfortable too. Just think about those times when you've found yourself averting your eyes because someone dropped a clanger on national TV.

_____

Imagine the camera is a friend

Don't be concerned if you suffer from stiffness during your first few attempts at recording: it's highly unnatural to speak to a small circle of glass. A time-honoured way to overcome this is to imagine having a conversation with a close friend instead of a camera. That might sound weird, but the psychology at play is much like the 'I am positive' method of dealing with nerves we examined above. This helps the brain to get into a more comfortable zone, causing the body to react accordingly. (This method certainly helps me a lot when I'm recording.)

_____

It's OK to look away

A final point to mention is that your Wonder Leads videos will be much improved if you look away occasionally from the camera. When holding a conversation, it's completely natural to look away at times rather than holding an intense gaze. Not only does this avoid the dreaded 'death stare' as mentioned earlier, it also shows that you are not reading from a script. It makes your video more impressive: that you genuinely know your stuff.

It's important to get the balance right, though. The vast majority of the time, be sure to keep a steady eye contact with the camera, especially when you are making a point: this builds a stronger connection with your prospect, reinforces your message and makes you appear more genuine.

ACTION POINTS

1. **Reframe negative emotions.** Tell yourself you are excited instead of nervous. Imagine the camera is a close friend instead of an inanimate object.
2. **Start and end with a smile and a wave.** Make sure your prospect knows that you are saying "Hello".
3. **Speak with feeling.** Vary pitch and tempo, and concentrate on delivering your words with confidence and friendliness, so that the prospect warms to you.
4. **Use positive gestures**. Contain uncontrolled mannerisms, and use body language to enhance your delivery.
5. **Feeling awkward is normal.** Don't worry if your first few recordings feel uncomfortable. The more recordings you do, the more natural it will become.

You've made it this far, so well done! You now have the tools, skills and knowledge to conquer the most challenging part of the entire Wonder Leads process: filming videos. Tenacity and willingness to overcome the unique personal challenges of recording in this way are the single biggest asset in generating leads for any business.

While this clears a big hurdle, your videos will need more time and attention before they're ready for the eyes of a prospect. Let's move on to *publishing*.

PART VI

PUBLISHING & MESSAGING

151

13

Introduction to Publishing

combination of relief, elation and – depending on how many videos have been filmed – exhaustion usually accompany a filming wrap. At this point we might be tempted to think the job done, but there's still plenty of important work ahead before our videos are ready to go.

They need to look right. They need to sound right. They also require a suitable home. These are all elements of publishing which can make or break a lead-generation push. Without further ado, let's look at the first task in this process: *editing*.

Editing

If our filming location has been set up correctly and the right equipment used, the sessions should have delivered the raw elements of a great video. The problem is, the footage is almost certainly a touch flawed. Inevitably, there will be pauses at the front while you get yourself ready, sections where you disappear off-camera at the end to check the footage. The audio is likely to be accompanied by the general hum of an office environment. The vocals might be too overpowering.

All of these can detract from our message. The good news is that Hollywood-style production skills aren't necessary: with the right software, editing is very simple, giving your video that perfect, professional polish in double-quick time.

1. DOWNLOAD THE FILES

The first step is to get the videos off the camera and onto a computer. This is usually a straightforward process involving software built into the computer, or supplied with the camera. Exact instructions vary, depending on your particular camera and computer, so it's best to check the process for your combination of devices.

Create an 'originals' folder

It is a good idea to save videos to a folder named 'originals' on your computer. This makes it easy to find the original footage, should there be a problem with the final exported file further down the line.

Use logical filenames for good version control

Once the Wonder Leads process is in full swing, the number of video files on your computer will quickly start to escalate, and it's crucial to be able to find the ones you want, when you want them. Unfortunately, default filenames from cameras don't help much, as they are usually non-descriptive – so, after you've downloaded your video files, replace the filenames with more logical ones.

The ideal format is to use firstname-surname-company, then add '_original' at the end so that it isn't mistaken for the final edited version. For example, if a camera stores movie files in mp4 format, an edited filename might look something like this:

joe-bloggs-acme-corporation_original.mp4

A clear, semantic filename makes locating individual videos much more efficient.

2. CHOOSE VIDEO EDITING SOFTWARE

The world of software moves at a rapid pace, so let's concentrate on the recommended features that any video editing software should include: this way, you can pick whichever is suitable for your operating system, technical knowledge and budget. A video editor must be able to do the following.

———

Trim footage

Our video needs to be kept as short as possible, cutting straight to the action, so the video editor must allow users to cut (trim) unwanted elements at the beginning and end of the original footage.

———

Remove background noise

Any audio recording outside of a soundproofed studio environment is likely to have a level of unwanted background noise: it sounds like a low hum, or sometimes like a rushing wind and makes the recording sound less professional, so being able to remove it is key.

———

Change audio level

Depending on where the mic is positioned, a voice may sound too loud or quiet during playback. This can be fixed so long as the video editor supports volume level adjustment.

———

Export optimised file sizes

Raw video files can be huge: for speed and efficiency during the editing and publishing process, it's important to reduce their size, as this cuts down storage needs and makes uploads speedier. As mentioned previously, 540px resolution and mp4 formats are worth looking out for, as they are optimised for faster web delivery.

And that's it! No doubt many video editors come with a range of incredible extra capabilities – they might be great, but they're not essential to create a great Wonder Leads video.

I'm a Mac user, so my go-to choice is iMovie – an excellent piece of software bundled with all modern Macs. It may lack the bells and whistles of more professional video editing software such as Final Cut or Adobe Premiere, but that doesn't matter. It does everything I need it to: it's simple to use, reliable and free! For me, that's a winning combination. If you're a PC user, the free Microsoft Windows Photos app does everything you need except removing background noise.1 Movie Maker has that feature, but it's old software no longer supported for updates by Microsoft. It can still be downloaded for free from the Microsoft website.

3. IMPORT AND TRIM THE FOOTAGE

Now we've chosen some editing software, it's time to work on the footage.

Trim the clip

After you've imported the original file into the editor, the next step is to trim it. Start by cutting the video so that it begins just before you say "Hello", and ends right after you say your final goodbye. Here are a couple of things to look out for.

Capture a smile and wave

Ideally, you want to be smiling and waving in the very first and very last frames of your video: the perfect frame is one where you appear happy, relaxed and natural.

For someone with a great face for radio like me, that can be a challenge. It's frustratingly easy to be caught midway through an expression change, or blurred while moving. Just move ('scrub') the playback marker until you locate a suitable starting frame – one that's as close as possible to the point immediately before the first word is spoken.

Don't leave a long gap at the start

If it isn't possible to find a decent frame right before the first word, scrub the playback slightly further until it is, but be careful of going too far back. If it takes longer than a second to find the right frame, it's fine to compromise with the best one available. We don't want the prospect to wait before the message starts playing, as this risks losing them. Your introduction will have much more impact if it goes straight into the action.

4. CLEAN UP THE AUDIO

Now you've trimmed the video, it's time to tidy up the sound.

Apply minimum noise reduction

For my introduction videos recorded in a typical office environment and edited using iMovie, I tend to impose anywhere from 60–90 per cent noise reduction: this figure varies from batch to batch, as the set-up and conditions of each filming session are different.

A video editor should be able to test how the audio sounds at each level, so do experiment until you find the level that works: the sweet spot is where all background noise has been removed, yet the voice isn't distorted. If it isn't possible to eliminate the noise without distortion, stop the reduction at the point where the voice is still clear. It's better to have a little background noise and a clear voice, than sounding like a robot.

Normalise audio levels

Depending on the speaking volume and mic position during recording, the sound level may need adjusting. This isn't critical, as there is no music or other sound to deal with, so prospects can always use the controls on their playback device to change the volume. However, if the recording is obviously too loud or quiet, it's sensible to adjust the audio levels to compensate.

Enhance your voice (optional)

Your video editor is likely to include a range of audio effects: these work in the same way as a graphic equaliser on a stereo, by altering treble and bass levels to place greater emphasis on certain tones.

While this step isn't essential, it can add clarity to a voice – which makes it easier for people to listen to. In iMovie, I use the 'Voice Enhance' audio profile; just experiment with the settings available in your chosen editor. As mentioned previously, the ideal result is sound where the voice has optimum clarity without distortion: if none of the available effects achieve that, it's better to leave the sound unaltered.

5. EXPORT THE FILE

Now you've finished editing, here are the next steps.

Find the exporting sweet spot

The export options available will depend on your video editor, so you will need to experiment a little when you first start, just to see which settings work best. Exported videos need an ideal combination of small file size and acceptable quality. If file size is reduced too much, the quality starts to deteriorate rapidly. If file size isn't sufficiently reduced, it will take a long time to upload and process.

> For my videos in iMovie, I use the 540px export profile with the 'High' quality setting applied. That produces a video file that is usually 20–30 per cent the size of the original raw version downloaded from my camera. As we've already identified, 540px video may not be as sharp as HD video when viewed full screen on a large desktop monitor, but it's still perfectly watchable.

Export with a logical filename

The final job is to make sure the filename is easily recognisable. Best practice dictates employing the same name for the edited videos as the original files, the only difference is omitting the '_original' from the end. For example:

joe-bloggs-acme-corporation.mp4

Create a separate folder, 'Edited', and move the edited file there: this makes it easier to compare the original and edited versions, and faster to locate the right video to attach to a landing page. (We'll be looking more at this in Chapter 14, 'Landing Pages').

6. TEST THE EXPORTED VIDEO

Compressing any kind of file can produce the occasional, unexpected result. To check for this, open the video and look it through quickly for sound and vision.

Check the filename corresponds to the prospect

As you're likely to be wearing the same clothes and standing in the same location for each batch of videos, this makes them easy to mix up. Run a check to ensure the name and company referenced in the recording corresponds to the video filename – essential to avoid embarrassment!

Check for corrupt footage

Scrub through the remaining footage quickly to ensure there are no gaps or unwanted elements. If there are, try a new export and retest. If problems persist, try adjusting the export settings, or refer to the 'help' section in the video editor documentation.

I once encountered a frustrating, intermittent issue where something was replacing parts of my footage with strange green bars. I didn't discover this until I had uploaded a video to my landing page. In the end, I traced the error back to an issue with my export settings, which meant I had to re-export all the affected videos.

If I had checked the videos immediately after exporting them, I would have saved myself a great deal of hassle.

This handy checklist will help you safely navigate the editing process.

VIDEO EDITING CHECKLIST

Download the files

- ❏ Transfer files from camera to computer
- ❏ Rename file: firstname-surname-company_ORIGINAL.XXX
- ❏ Place in an 'Originals' folder

Choose a video editor

- ❏ Allows trimming
- ❏ Allows background noise removal
- ❏ Allows audio level changes
- ❏ Allows file export optimisation

Import and trim the footage

- ❏ Import footage to editor
- ❏ Trim start to point just before speaking starts (waving and smiling normally)
- ❏ Trim end of clip to just after closing remark (waving and smiling normally)

Clean up the audio

- ❏ Apply minimum noise reduction
- ❏ Normalise audio levels
- ❏ Enhance voice if required

Export the file

- ❏ Find your exporting sweet spot (540px resolution)
- ❏ Name the exported file as: firstname-surname-company.XXX
- ❏ Place in an 'Edited' folder

Test your exported video

- ❏ Check the filename matches the prospect
- ❏ Check playback quality
- ❏ Check for corrupt footage

ACTION POINTS

1. **Choose a usable editor.** Don't be seduced by elaborate features and functionality. So long as a video editor can do the essentials well, that's all that matters.
2. **Note all your settings.** The first time you go through the process, it will take a while to find the best settings. After that, just repeat the same editing steps for every video.
3. **Keep your edits subtle.** Resist the temptation to modify your video too much or add additional effects. You don't want to detract from your message.
4. **Keep everything organised.** Clear, logical filenames and folders make it easier to find the videos you need, as the number of introductions grows.
5. **Test, test, test.** Save yourself time in the long run by double-checking every video for errors and correct filenames.
6. **Use the Wonder Leads Video Editing Checklist** to walk you through the recommended steps.

With video editing safely navigated, your next step is building somewhere for it to live: a *landing page*.

14

Landing Pages

A **'landing page' is the term** given to a web page optimised for visitors looking for specific content. Usually it's an entry point to a website from another online location, such as a search results page or link from another site, but it can be linked from offline sources too.

Landing pages should serve two primary purposes:

- Engage the user with valuable content relevant to what they were expecting before visiting
- Encourage users to continue their digital journey through clear calls to action

Let's look at the make-up of a perfect Wonder Leads landing page.

What makes a great landing page?

The best way to understand what makes a good Wonder Leads landing page is to dissect the main components (Figure 4).

1. BRANDING

Your personal introduction to your prospect is also on behalf of your business, so the landing page should display your company branding in its colours, and feature the logo near the top of the page. When your prospect visits the page, they will start to build brand recognition and make the association between you and your business.

2. VIDEO PLAYER

The player for the introductory video is the most critical part of a landing page: the prominent visual element. To ensure the prospect focuses on your content, strip the player controls back to all but the essential features:

- Thumbnail image
- Prominent play button
- Volume control
- 'Full screen' button
- Progress bar.

– anything else simply causes distraction

3. PERSONAL GREETING

The goal of a Wonder Leads landing page is getting the prospect to click the 'play' button. The video thumbnail features the prospect's name and company (more on this in 'Video thumbnail' below), but it won't draw them in alone.

To make them more comfortable about clicking ahead, simply include a short personal greeting at the top of the page: "Hello Steve" or "Hi Pascale" is perfectly fine. (Again here, just be sure to check appropriate etiquette and cultural differences, adapting to individual prospects during international introductions.)

4. POSITIONING STATEMENT

The next task is to reinforce the video's purpose. We recently asked them to connect on LinkedIn, and luckily for us they accepted: they could have ignored the approach and gone merrily on with their working day, but they didn't. As they've granted us access to their professional world, "Thanks for connecting with me!" sets the tone for the video content.

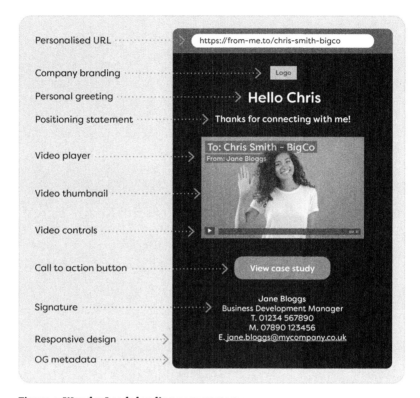

Figure 4: Wonder Leads landing page anatomy

5. CALL-TO-ACTION BUTTON

As we've discussed, the case study plays a central role in any Wonder Leads script, so we want to make it easy to access. Underneath your video, place a call-to-action button that links to the case study: it should stand out visually from other elements on the page, with clear text: for example, 'View case study'. Keep the button text succinct: when it contains too many words, it looks odd and makes the design less professional.

6. SIGNATURE

While the prospect has your LinkedIn details already, they're unlikely to have your primary contact details. We want to make it easy for them to get in touch, so the last visual element of the page is a signature block.

Treat this much like an email signature, including a suitably respectful sign-off, with:

- Your name
- Job title and company name
- Email address
- Business phone number
- Mobile number (optional)

There is another advantage to putting your contact details on a landing page: if your prospect shares the link to the landing page, then anyone who views it can also contact you direct.

Caveat: do check that any information you include is suitable for public access.

7. RESPONSIVE DESIGN

According to statistics published by LinkedIn[1], mobile devices account for 57 per cent of all site visits. For that reason, your landing page must be responsive and look just as good on a smartphone as it does on a desktop computer. (This is why we keep landing page content to a minimum: the video can end up being pushed off-screen on smaller devices by too much text. That would be a disaster, and almost certainly result in far fewer views.)

8. OPEN GRAPH TAGS

Website metadata describe web page content for other websites that might reference that content. For example, meta-title and meta-description tags are used by search engines such as Google to help them understand both the importance of web pages, and what summary information to display in their search results. Metadata is also used by LinkedIn to build previews of weblinks that are shared within the platform.

The type of metadata used by LinkedIn is an Open Graph (OG) tag. There are various types of OG tag that control the content that appears when a link is shared on LinkedIn: for example, its preview image and title. Depending on how your landing pages have been built (we'll be discussing this shortly in 'Hosting your landing pages'), it may be possible to customise the OG tag data for your landing page, to maximise the impact of the initial sharing message. We'll be looking at that further in Chapter 15, but for now it's simply important to understand the five OG tags that should be integrated, and the content they need to display:

1. **og:url** – the URL of the landing page
2. **og:title** – your personal greeting, e.g. "Hello Chris!"
3. **og:description** – positioning statement, e.g. "Thanks for connecting with me."
4. **og:image** – your introduction video thumbnail
5. **og:type** – set to 'image' (instead of the more obvious 'video', because otherwise the thumbnail will be obscured by a 'play' button when we share it).

There are lots of other OG tags available, but they aren't required for Wonder Leads landing pages.[**]

Video thumbnail

This is a critical component that deserves special attention. The thumbnail is displayed until the prospect clicks 'play', and plays a big part in driving them to the video in the first place (as we will see in Chapter 15), so it needs to draw them in.

The perfect thumbnail should match a still frame from the video where you're waving and smiling naturally: it could be the first frame. As with your video, this is a friendly, quotable, "hello" gesture

**For details of how to format these tags properly within the html of a landing page, refer to the Open Graph website: ogp.me

that doesn't require speech to be understood. Overlaid on the thumbnail image – being careful not to obscure your face – should be the prospect's name and company, and your name underneath.

This is crucial, because if your prospect hasn't experienced a Wonder Leads approach before, they may be sceptical when it lands in their inbox. By adding their name and company to the thumbnail, their thought process is changed completely, instantly becoming more engaged. Why? Well, it all comes down to some fundamental human psychology.

> The need for individual recognition is an integral part of 'esteem': the fourth level of Abraham Maslow's Hierarchy of Needs.[2] To this day, Maslow's landmark 1943 research into the psychology of human motivation remains a popular framework in the highest academic circles. Maslow proposed that most people require stable self-respect and self-esteem: an essential part of this is a need for respect from others, including status, recognition, prestige and attention.

Taking the time to display the prospect's name and company is a visible gesture of respect, which elevates their feeling of self-importance and fulfils one of their basic human desires. That's an impressive amount of positive psychology from one seemingly trivial design detail.

Hosting your landing pages

Now we've seen how a landing page should look, we need to make it accessible to prospects – which means choosing a website or platform to host it. Let's look at some of the main options available

1. YOUTUBE OR VIMEO

The first thought that enters most people's heads is YouTube or

Vimeo, and these options are indeed good for anyone in a rush, without access to any technical resources or budget:

- They offer free accounts – each video has its own page with a unique, shareable link.
- They are globally recognised – prospects are likely to have viewed content on those platforms, and will be familiar with their interfaces.
- They include in-built editing – reducing the need for a video editor. (It's even possible to embed call-to-action buttons to attract more clicks, although this usually requires a paid plan.)

When I started my Wonder Leads journey, I gave a lot of thought to using one of these platforms, because in theory, they were ideal: cheap, robust, globally recognised. It seemed a no-brainer.

In reality, they were both wide of the mark. The main reason was lack of customisation: I wanted everything on my landing page to look a specific way, designed to encourage clicks and generate leads. While YouTube and Vimeo are brilliant platforms, they were built to serve a completely different purpose: sharing videos to as many people as possible.

Wonder Leads is designed to be shared person-to-person, as a bespoke communication. While YouTube and Vimeo videos can be set to 'private' – i.e. they won't show up in online search results – the functionality was still flawed for my purposes. Neither offered the level of personalisation I needed. Both landing pages were more about Vimeo and YouTube than my business. Of course: they want users and customers to stay on their platform, view more videos and sign up to their services. Because of that, their brand is always going to be the main draw.

I wanted my prospects to visit my landing page and feel like it's a natural extension of my business. Neither platform allowed me to do that.

If none of this sounds like a problem, and you do want to take the YouTube or Vimeo route, here are a few things to consider.

Use a custom URL

First, you'll need a service to change the default YouTube and Vimeo landing page links into personalised ones for each recipient. By default, both platforms identify each video using a unique series of letters and numbers: if that is shared, the prospect will have no idea that the destination contains personalised content – significantly reducing the chances of getting them to click.

If it isn't possible to change the URL within the platform, you may need to consider using a shortening service like Bitly (Bitly.com) to create custom URLs which can be shared. (We'll be looking at URLs in more detail in the next section.)

Prevent ads from showing

Second, it's important to stop as much third-party content appearing on your landing pages as possible. This is a challenge on YouTube, where adverts and suggested videos pour out of every digital orifice. Vimeo is more stripped back, but limiting the number of related videos and surplus content showing on the page is still key.

Every unwanted element has the potential to distract your prospect and prevent them from viewing your video.

Make sure your video starts immediately

Third, when a prospect clicks 'play', the video needs to start immediately. On YouTube, anyone watching a video who isn't logged in as a 'Premium' member could find themselves sitting through a third-party advert before it plays. That does plenty of harm to anybody's lead-generation statistics.

Vimeo has a much stricter advertising policy, so users never get an advert before a video, but playlists to other videos still appear – especially at the end of a video, and possibly on the landing page too.

Be sure to check precisely what content a prospect is likely to see when viewing your landing page, so they don't encounter something that lessens its impact (like an introduction to another prospect, for example!).

2. YOUR WEBSITE

An alternative to YouTube and Vimeo is to create landing pages on your own website: there are several benefits to doing this.

Design freedom
There are no design restrictions. Using your company website gives you complete control over every detail of the landing page – from logo size to video placement.

Promotes your brand
This route offers excellent brand recognition. Using Vimeo or YouTube for Wonder Leads landing pages means the YouTube or Vimeo brand taking precedence over your logo, site navigation and the URL. Using a company site allows your branding to shine through without being diluted.

Improved continuation
If the prospect is already on your company's website, clicking through to a case study on the same site offers a seamless user experience.

Easy data analysis
Combined with a platform such as Google Analytics, detailed reports can be available to show you which landing pages are receiving views: this is essential for both monitoring and evaluating activity, and improving subsequent approaches (more on this in Part VII: Measuring).

For all the above reasons, a landing page on a company website is a far better option than one hosted on Vimeo or YouTube. But there are still a few downsides to consider.

Hiring a web designer

Unless you have coding skills, you'll need to hire a designer/developer to create the landing pages and build this functionality into your website.

Hosting video files elsewhere

Hosting video on your company website is a bad idea: it eats up storage space and kills server bandwidth, grinding your visitors' experience to a halt. Instead, it's best to host videos on a third-party service which can be embedded in your company site.

Vimeo and YouTube are both suitable: it simply requires setting your videos to private, and restricting the embedding to a specific website (namely, yours).

> When I started, I used Vimeo to host my video files, then embedded them into each landing page. The main reason I chose Vimeo instead of YouTube is that the player looks far more professional, and I found it simpler to remove the ads.
>
> The main downside to doing this is time. You have to upload the video to Vimeo, then create the rest of the landing page separately within your website, juggling two services.
>
> While I managed to do this for a while, it added a significant extra step to every introduction I wanted to create.

Integrating analytics

As well as a video hosting service, third-party analytics software is required to track engagements. (I use Google Analytics for my website. It's a brilliant system – free and full of incredible features.) However, it's yet another data source to monitor regularly.

Long URLs

Using a company website means heavy reliance on the length of its domain name. If the company domain name is long, then sharing links will end up being *very* long, which poses additional problems by making reading more difficult.

Ideally, a sharing URL should be as short as possible.

Domain restrictions

Using a company website keeps things locked to that single domain. That's fine if a company only has a single site, but if it has multiple websites – perhaps for different products or services – independent landing page functionality is needed for each site. That could quickly become difficult to manage.

The next hosting solution offers a simple workaround for all of this: Socialaser.

3. SOCIALASER

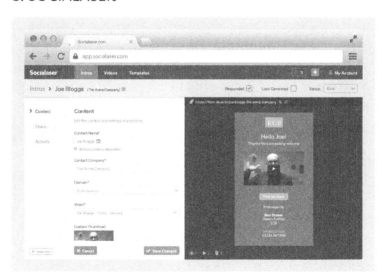

Socialaser is a cloud-based software application developed specifically to run and manage lead-generation activities using the Wonder Leads method. The system has a purpose-built template editor, video hosting, one-click message-sharing and powerful reporting built into a single, intuitive web interface. All the learning gained while creating the Wonder Leads process has been poured into the development of Socialaser. The software aims to make the Wonder Leads methodology accessible to anyone, regardless of their technical knowledge, location and experience.

Socialaser:

- Shows critical performance specific to Wonder Leads, such as lead generation rates, response rates and the most successful scripts
- Supports multiple sending domains
- Can integrate easily with an existing company website
- Integrates with special custom domains, taking personalisation to another level
- Is in constant development, releasing new features and time-saving shortcuts

Not only can a landing page be operational within seconds, but compared with managing landing pages on a website, administration time can be reduced by up to 50 per cent. That means a lot less time managing the process, and a lot more time generating leads.

You can start using Socialaser for free. So, if you want your Wonder Leads to hit the ground running, it could be worth a look. Check out wonderleads.com/socialaser for details.

Landing page URL

As we've established, your URL is crucial to the design, driving prospects to your landing page.

1. THE PROBLEM WITH OBSCURE LINKS

If Vimeo is selected for the landing page, the default sharing URL for a video looks something like this:

https://vimeo.com/65102146

For YouTube, it looks even more obscure:

https://www.youtube.com/watch?v=tTjHEyEAlsc

We're all familiar with that style of link, and no doubt we've clicked many in our time. The problem is, obscure links give no indication of what might be lurking on the other side. That all changes when we use a personalised URL.

2. THE BENEFITS OF PERSONALISED URLS

Sometimes referred to as a 'vanity' or 'branded' URL, a personalised URL is one where the text visibly relates to the content being shared.

> The impact of using a personalised URL is enormous. A 2015 study by Bitly,[3] the global leader in URL shortening, found that branded URLs can increase click-through rates by up to 34 per cent compared with unbranded links.

Whatever the domain name, be sure to personalise the customisable portion of the URL (the 'slug') with the prospect's name and company. Present it all in lower case, with hyphens between each word for readability, for example:

https://yoursite.com/joe-bloggs-acme-company

This also gives you a personalised, shareable link, benefiting from the positive effects outlined by Maslow's Hierarchy of Needs.

With Socialaser, I've achieved functionality that customises the way my URLs look on every level. While I still have the option of using my company domain, I can also use a range of entirely different domain names that I've registered and integrated with my account.

My current personal favourite is my 'from-dave.to' domain: '.to' is the top-level domain for Tonga, but it can be registered by users outside of the country too. Having this domain means that my links now look like this:

https://from-dave.to/joe-bloggs-acme-company

Not only is this link structure far more concise, but the page function as a friendly, direct message to the recipient is almost universally understood, at least in English-speaking cultures. While the reference to my company has gone, this isn't necessarily a bad thing. It makes my approach seem more personal and less like run-of-the-mill business marketing, which is precisely what the Wonder Leads framework is all about.

We can appreciate how significant this attention to detail is by analysing the statistics from my Wonder Leads approaches. Every introduction incorporated a personalised URL. As previously stated, just over half of all the introductions were viewed: from those views, 80 per cent created a response, and one in every five of those responses generated a lead. As the goal is to generate as many leads as possible, our immediate thought might be to create as many videos as possible – that will help, but it isn't the most efficient use of time.

> *The best way to generate more leads is to improve the view rate.*

Personalising the URL is one of the best methods available to help achieve that.

ACTION POINTS

1. **Don't overcomplicate the design.** The more streamlined your landing page, the more your video will shine.
2. **Offer a personalised experience.** Use personalised titles, greeting, URLs, thumbnails and OG tags to make your landing pages feel bespoke.
3. **Choose the right system.** Select one to host your landing pages that suits your budget, technical knowledge and time constraints.
4. **Use the Wonder Leads Landing Page Anatomy** for reference when constructing your landing page design.

15

Introduction to Messaging

You've now successfully navigated the most technically challenging parts of the Wonder Leads framework! While the bulk of that work is done, there are still some important things to consider. In this chapter, we'll be looking at generating the highest possible number of video views by structuring our message.

Initial sharing message

As you'll have seen, we've made a great deal of effort already to reach this point. We've connected with a relevant prospect, recorded an engaging video introduction, created a compelling landing page, and are now ready to make our approach. The problem is, it'll all be for nothing if we can't get our prospect to the landing page.

Here, the initial sharing message is key: if your prospects don't click to your video, the lead is a dead duck. *How* we make the introduction is almost as important as *what* is in it.

WHY SHARING MUST BE POSITIVE

Have you ever received a message from someone through LinkedIn and it's clear that they have not given one iota of thought to how badly they might be perceived? If you're anything like me, the answer is a categoric 'Yes!' These messages usually follow the same, predictably sad format:

> Hi Dave – Managing Director, how's it going, friend?
> I've been working on something totally mind-blowing. It's a unique invention that no one else knows about. It will literally save you hundreds of millions of pounds overnight.
> The window for using it expires tomorrow, so don't be a loser and miss out, or your business is probably going to go under.
> You can find out everything you need to know in this pathetic marketing leaflet which I couldn't even be bothered to format properly. Oh, and you'll need to download it from this random web address. You'll just need to enter in all your credit card details first. In fact, it doesn't really matter if you fill the form in or not, because I've already got all your contact details from this dodgy database I bought online.
> So don't worry, I'll email you 20 minutes after I've sent this message, then I'll call you at home tomorrow. 7am all right?
> *~ Doug*

Of course, I'm exaggerating things a touch here, but the sentiment of many messages flying about on LinkedIn is much the same: 'Me, me, me.' What's the recipient's response? 'Delete, delete, delete.'

How well we communicate a message plays a huge part in how well it is received, so it's worth taking the time to get this right. It's a significant challenge, balancing the prospect's preferences with our desire to promote our business. An overriding thought might be that the prospect might not prefer to hear from us at all, but we need to put that to one side.

> Imagine this scenario: you and I meet for the first time at an industry event that we're both attending independently. We sit next to each other, so I say "Hello", and you say "Hello" back. We ask each other about our companies, exchange some pleasantries about the speakers, then settle in to watch the proceedings.

> And that's the end of our interaction – until we end up sitting opposite each other during lunch. Now, what happens? We continue our conversation, of course; only this time, we share a few more details and learn about each other.

Through connecting, the early stages of a conversation have already begun: reaching out and responding in kind. Your prospect may not have used words as they might face-to-face, but they have implied the sentiment in accepting the connection. Think of it as a virtual tip of the hat.

Consider this: your response to that virtual gesture hasn't been to scurry back to the comfort of anonymity, like 99 per cent of all new social media connections. Instead, you have gone away and invested valuable time and effort to craft a brilliant piece of personalised communication, *just for them*. You're simply taking the first brave step to ignite the second phase of the conversation.

Returning to our event analogy, this is like following up on our earlier chit-chat by seeing you in the lunch queue, buying it for you, carrying it to your table and giving you a pass to the VIP area for good measure. After going to all that effort, there's a pretty good chance that you'll warm to me a little more than you otherwise would. At least you wouldn't be unhappy. What reason would you have?

Now we've established why sharing is advantageous, all we need is a suitable structure to action it: this is where the Seven Cs come in.

THE SEVEN CS OF COMMUNICATION

In 1990, an article in the *Washington Post* stated, 'if there is such a thing as the 10 commandments of business, then the second was laid down by Scott M. Cutlip and Allen H. Center'.[1] The article was referring to the famous 'Seven Cs of Communication', which Cutlip and Center outlined in their 1952 book, *Effective Public Relations*.[2] Still widely referenced today (although often not in its original form), the Seven Cs describe the necessary elements of effective communication. Here they are, with a definition relating to message-sharing:

- **Complete** – say everything you need
- **Concise** – keep it short
- **Considerate** – put yourself in your prospect's shoes
- **Concrete** – make the purpose clear
- **Courteous** – treat the prospect with respect
- **Clear** – don't try to hide anything
- **Correct** – don't make any mistakes

These are excellent rules of thumb for composing a sharing message. They are also brilliant guidelines to follow when communicating positively with another person – and when it comes to Wonder Leads, that means every time.

Let's break down how they can help to shape an initial sharing message, step-by-step.

Initial sharing message structure

The ideal Wonder Leads initial sharing message follows many of the same principles that guide the structure of a video script (see Chapter 9, 'Building a Wonder Leads script'). Here's the best way to structure for maximum effectiveness:

1. OPENING

First, reopen the conversation with a positive greeting. Now your prospect is a new connection, acknowledging how happy you are to be acquainted is a perfect step, because it shows you value the relationship. For example: "Hi Rob, it's great to be connected." It's concise, courteous and sets the tone for what's to follow.

2. POSITIONING

Now the conversation has been reignited, we need to explain why, and consider the benefits to the prospect. One of the biggest challenges of social media is that it isn't actually that social. People regularly make hundreds, thousands, even millions of connections, but afterwards they remain anonymous to one another. A person may follow the other's activity, but there is no mutual conversation or anything to build a meaningful relationship.

The primary advantage of Wonder Leads to a prospect is that the video enables them to get to know the sender a little better in a short amount of time. It becomes far more important than a simple lead-generation tool: it offers relationship-building with genuine mutual value. How often can that be said about social media?

The best approach to positioning your video is to acknowledge this sentiment upfront, for example: "Rather than be another anonymous face in your network, I thought it would be nicer to say 'Hello' personally. So I've recorded a quick video, just for you..."

It's clear, concise, considerate and concrete. Best of all, it's a statement that anyone should feel proud to write.

3. SHARING LINK

Now the message has a proper frame, all that's left is to add the hyperlink to the landing page, for example:

https://from-dave.to/joe-bloggs-acme-company

A personalised URL like this ticks all of the Seven Cs with just 44 little characters.

4. LINK PREVIEW

Remember the OG metadata that we added to the landing page in Chapter 14? Well, now is where it counts. Whenever a hyperlink is inserted into a LinkedIn message, it generates a preview of the web page using the OG tags embedded within the source page. So long as the OG tags have been set up correctly, the preview will display the greeting, positioning statement and crucially, the video thumbnail.

> According to a study by Forbes Insights,[3] given a choice, 59 per cent of company decision-makers would rather watch a video than read an article or blog post.
>
> That means prospects are more likely to engage with a message if it links visibly to a video, rather than a standard web page.

The only thing to bear in mind is that LinkedIn doesn't display the preview until *after* the message has been posted, so we need to be 100 per cent sure that the embedded metadata is accurate before hitting 'send'. If the message isn't checked properly beforehand, it's easy to end up sharing it with an incorrect preview: for this reason, when you're starting out, it's a good idea to send a test message to a friend or colleague who can check that the preview is correctly formatted.

The reason this matters is because even though it is finally possible to edit or delete LinkedIn messages[4], you must assume the prospect will read it immediately.

Of course, we all know that perception is everything. Mistakes in a sharing message, no matter how small, sow seeds of doubt about the quality of a person's work, so being on the ball is vital. The devil may well be in the detail, but the long-term rewards are too.

When I first used landing pages on my website, generating these previews was a pain. I had to create individual thumbnails for the image preview, and write my meta-title and description tags separately. Not only did this add to the time it took to create each introduction, but it also meant an even higher chance of error.

Thankfully I now have Socialaser, which automates all of these processes. It saves time and minimises potentially embarrassing episodes.

5. CLOSE

A simple close is definitely the best way to end an initial sharing message: we don't want to overstay our welcome. A short, polite sign-off does everything you need, for example: "Kind regards, Jackson". It's clear, concrete and concise, and keeps the tone both professional and cordial.

When complete, your initial sharing message can look something like this – feel free to customise it and make it your own.

INITIAL SHARING MESSAGE TEMPLATE

Hi [PROSPECT NAME],

It's great to be connected with you.

Rather than be another anonymous face in your network, I thought it would be nicer to say hello personally. So I've recorded a quick video just for you...

[SHARING LINK]

Kind regards,

[YOUR NAME]

Timing the initial sharing message

If you're a bit of a statistics nerd like me, you might be wondering if there's an optimum time to send your sharing message to get responses from prospects. As it turns out, there might well be (Figure 5).

I kept a log of all the highly positive responses that I received from my approaches: that is, where the prospect specifically praised the quality of my communication. The average time it took to receive a positive response from making an initial connection was four days, indicating that prospects are most impressed if a sharing message is sent shortly after connecting. *My guidance would be to aim to share your video within a week for maximum impact.*

Of all the replies received, 49 per cent were direct responses to my initial sharing message. The most popular day to receive a first-time response from a prospect (i.e. one that didn't require a follow-up communication) was Wednesday. I received just over 35 per cent of all replies that day. On average, it took a prospect 1.1 days from receiving their sharing message to send their first-time response.

Based on this evidence, the best day to send a message to maximise your chance of a first-time reply is Tuesday.

Figure 5: First-time response to initial sharing message, by day

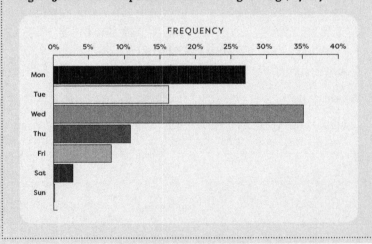

These are certainly not hard-and-fast rules, so don't worry too much if you can't adhere to them. For example, I've received a highly positive response 18 days after making an initial connection, so it isn't critical to send yours within four days. Geographic location and industry are likely to make a significant difference here too. All the businesses I targeted were in the UK manufacturing sector; you are likely to have different preferences, based on the location and industry you're targeting.

The best thing is to experiment to find the schedule that works well for you.

ACTION POINTS

1. **Don't rush it.** The success of Wonder Leads hangs on getting people to view the video. Make sure your message is the best it can be.
2. **Use the Seven Cs.** Check that your message adheres to the principles of positive and effective communication.
3. **Check the preview.** Send a test message to a friend or colleague who can send you a screenshot of how your preview looks from their end.
4. **Double-check your content.** Once your sharing message has been sent in LinkedIn, assume it will be read by the prospect straight away. Don't let the whole approach fall flat through sloppy execution.
5. **Act fast.** Share your message within a week of connecting for maximum impact.
6. **Use the Wonder Leads Initial Sharing Message Template** to get you started.

16

Follow-up Message

Pressing 'send' on your initial sharing message is a massive step: a culmination of all the energy you've put into Wonder Leads so far. After the effort that's gone into the video, it still might not be enough to elicit a response. To have the best chance of starting that all-important conversation with a prospect, we need to follow up. Let's walk through how to ace it.

The art of the follow-up

Don't you just hate it when a salesperson repeatedly pesters you to find out whether you've read their message? It usually happens about two days after their first approach:

> Hey Dave,
> Did you have a chance to see my last message? I know I've already said it, but I think this will be PERFECT for you. It's going to change the way you do business FOREVER.
> Your competitors are already using it, so whatever you do, DON'T be the mug who's last to the party. Let's meet up, and I will explain everything.
> ~ Jane

If you're as unfortunate as me, variations of that message land in your inbox every week (and they probably will for the rest of time). There are three significant problems with this approach.

1. No empathy

The first, as we discussed in Chapter 15, is that it's self-centred: all the seller does is talk about what they think and how great they think their business is. This assumes that the prospect *has* to be interested, and that meeting up is an *inevitability*. The prospect might have read the first message. It may even have got their attention. But it probably isn't a priority to them now.

A follow-up like this just tells the prospect that the sender has no consideration for them whatsoever – so why should they give anything back?

2. No value

The second is that it doesn't offer any new value. Many follow-up messages simply repeat most of the first email. If a prospect doesn't respond to the initial email after reading it, why would they reply to another one saying exactly the same thing?

3. No patience

The final one is timing: two or three days after the first message simply isn't long enough to wait before sending a follow-up. In all probability, the prospect won't have even read the first one yet. They might be working away, or be on holiday. They might even be prioritising work over checking messages from someone they barely know on LinkedIn.

I know – how very dare they!

The empathy gap

There's a significant disparity between what most sellers and buyers think. It would appear the reason can be traced back to what psychologists call 'the empathy gap'.

In a 2016 HubSpot survey,[1] a group of buyers were asked to submit the word they most associated with salespeople: the answer was 'pushy'. That's unlikely to be a major surprise to anyone, but the research did shed further light on the potential source of the problem.

When asked how they approach buyers, 50 per cent of surveyed sellers said they avoid being pushy; but 84 per cent of buyers who have had a neutral or negative experience with sales said that sellers were pushy.

In 2015, a study led by Dr Irene Scopelliti, Senior Lecturer in Marketing at City, University of London,[2] set out to prove why recipients of self-promotion often viewed such activity as 'bragging' and consequently deemed self-promoters less likeable.

In a series of controlled experiments, the researchers split participants into two groups: 'Self-Promoters' and 'Recipients'. They asked the Self-Promoters to engage in several tasks where they would demonstrate self-promotional behaviour in front of the Recipients. The researchers then asked the Self-Promoters to rate the emotional response they expected to have elicited from the Recipients. The researchers compared those ratings with the emotional reactions that the Recipients scored themselves.

The study found that Self-Promoters consistently overestimated the extent to which self-promotion elicits positive emotions, while underestimating how much it evokes negative emotions. And not just a little bit – they were off by *huge* margins.

Scopelliti writes: 'As a consequence, when seeking to maximize the favourability of the opinion others have of them, people engage in excessive self-promotion that has the opposite of its intended effects'.

> What reason does she cite? 'The difficulty in engaging in emotional perspective-taking.' In other words, the empathy gap.

These results go a long way to explaining why we all get so insanely annoyed by overly persistent salespeople. They might think they're being helpful, but we simply see them as bragging, and so our opinion of them diminishes. The more they self-promote, the less likeable they become.

Every self-serving follow-up message that comes through simply serves to bang another nail in the coffin of our fledgling relationships.

A radical approach to follow-ups

> I was lucky the first time I shared a batch of introductions: I received some extremely positive replies straightaway.
>
> If you're starting from scratch, you may not enjoy the same fortune of an immediate reply, but that's OK. It's entirely normal not to get an answer to an initial sharing message: only 47 per cent of the responses I received came back first time. The rest have been in response to a *follow-up*.

By now, it should be clear that Wonder Leads is a framework based on *positive* human relationships: the last thing it was designed for was to annoy someone. For that reason, we only check to see if someone has seen their video *once*. After that, we quietly accept the fact that the prospect is most likely not interested, and gracefully move on to the next. There are always more suitable fish in the sea, especially when quality comes before quantity.

I appreciate that this advice might fly in the face of almost every sales book that's been written: 'follow up or die' being the oft-quoted mantra of the seasoned sales professional. For example, a CEO of a leading sales website explains that if prospects say they aren't interested, he lets them be. But if they don't respond, he advocates following up until they do, citing an occasion where a prospect was contacted *48 times* before successfully arranging a meeting.[3]

That's a pretty staggering display of persistence. While it may work with a small percentage of prospects, it ends up alienating everyone else. Some people just don't want to reply, and that's entirely their prerogative. The objective here is not just to generate a business opportunity, but to nurture *meaningful* professional relationships that pay greater rewards over the long term. It's simply not possible to achieve that by bombarding prospects with messages, or pleading with them to engage. It actively pushes people away and undermines value by making sellers look desperate.

> *The ideal B2B follow-up should play the long game, showing humility and respect for the recipient.*

With that in mind, we aren't even going to call it a 'follow-up'. Instead, let's call it a 'nudge'.

Nudge message structure

The definition of a nudge is a friendly, well-meaning gesture designed to elicit a reaction. A Wonder Leads nudge is a short message sent to a prospect, a *considered* amount of time after sending the initial share. It should be sent to anyone who did not respond originally, regardless of whether they viewed the video or not. A nudge serves three purposes:

1. Encourages prospects to view the video
2. Gets a response from those who have viewed it
3. Shows an ability to bridge the empathy gap

A nudge is a more relaxed style of message. All social media platforms – even LinkedIn – are first and foremost, conversational platforms, so formal etiquette isn't always necessary. In fact, prospects are likely to warm to you more if you can let your professional guard down in subtle, yet meaningful, ways.

Let's look at how to construct a good nudge.

1. OPENING

Make your greeting short and friendly, and use the prospect's first name. It's a good idea to vary this from the original sharing message, because it makes them visibly different within LinkedIn. If "Hi Rob" was used in the initial sharing message, then "Hello Rob" might be a choice start to a nudge.

2. QUESTION

For the nudge to meet our first objective, we need to ask the prospect if they've seen the video. How we phrase that question is important. We could simply say, "Did you see the video I sent you?", but this is a direct, closed question demanding a binary response – yes or no – and puts our prospect on the spot. Because we don't yet have the strength in our relationship to get away with such directness, they're more likely to ignore us.

It's far better to ask a more friendly, open-ended question, such as: "I hope you managed to view the video I recorded for you OK?" It makes prospects feel more comfortable, because it offers them flexibility in their response. Referring to the video "I" recorded for "you" also reminds them that the content has been created just for them: this should help to spark their interest, in case they've overlooked that detail first time around.

3. SPARK INTRIGUE

At this point, try and generate further curiosity. A personalised video introduction is quite an unusual way of contacting someone, but it offers way more value to the recipient. This novelty factor can be put to good use by making a statement such as: "Slightly unorthodox, I know, but hopefully a bit more useful!"

The idea with such an approach is that prospect asks themselves: "Why is it unorthodox?", "Why is it more useful?" If they start asking these questions, they're more inclined to revisit the previous message and click the link.

4. OFFER HELP

The big problem with technology is being sure that it actually works. There could be umpteen reasons why a prospect hasn't viewed a video: maybe it didn't play or the link didn't work; perhaps the sound didn't come through or the picture kept breaking up.

These can and do occur from time to time, so this is a perfect opportunity to offer assistance, for example: "Let me know if you had any technical trouble, and I'll see if I can help." This statement adds value to the conversation and shows a willingness to overcome challenges – one of the main characteristics any buyer looks for in a new supplier.

5. CLOSE

The final step is bringing the message to a suitable conclusion. This time, simply use your first name rather than a sign-off, so the message feels more like a note and less like a formal approach.

Try using this template to help get you started – feel free to alter it to your own style.

NUDGE MESSAGE TEMPLATE

Hi [PROSPECT NAME],

I hope you managed to view the video I recorded for you OK?

Slightly unorthodox I know, but hopefully a bit more useful!

Let me know if you had any technical trouble and I'll see if I can help.

[YOUR NAME]

Timing your nudges

After sharing your first batch of Wonder Leads videos, naturally you'll be eager to get results – you've invested a lot of time and energy to reach this point, but it's also key to time your nudge right.

If it's timed wrongly, it risks alienating the prospect; if it's well-timed, the prospect will regard the sender more highly. What defines it is patience: the more time that can be left between a sharing message and a nudge, the better. We are not talking about leaving it for months, but it's worth remembering the real enemy we're trying to regale against: everything average. If the standard sales follow-up comes three to seven days after the first contact, it makes sense to try something different. Something that shows we are *better*.

Why not double that time, or triple it? Heck, why not even leave it a month – what's the worst that can happen? Will the prospect be distraught that they haven't been contacted again? No. Will a sales opportunity have been lost because the window has closed? Unlikely. Remember, most B2B buying windows appear infrequently, which is why Wonder Leads has been designed to help businesses succeed *over the long term*.

In reality, the only thing that delaying a nudge means is having to wait a little longer to start seeing results. In the meantime, there will be opportunities to continue building more connections, create more videos and share more introductions to fill the Wonder Leads pipeline. As soon as nudges start going out, they will continue to go out on a recurring basis, just as any good follow-up programme should.

Nudges *really* work. In my experience, 43 per cent of all responses are as a result of a nudge. Not only are they successful in getting prospects to view the video for the first time, but they also encourage people who had seen the video but not yet responded, to send a reply. The average time it took my prospects to respond to a nudge was just 2.2 days.

If you can hold your nerve, the benefits should come your way soon enough.

ACTION POINTS

1. **Be patient.** Leave your nudge for a minimum of two weeks, but aim for four if you can. It will have all the more power for it.
2. **Make it helpful.** Show empathy by offering support to overcome any problems they might have encountered.
3. **Keep it brief.** Make your nudge as short as possible, and friendly.
4. **Follow up once.** Play the long game by keeping prospects on-side. It also stops you from appearing desperate.
5. **Use the Wonder Leads Nudge Message Template** to get you started – customise it to suit your own style.

17

Insight Sharing Message

As we discussed in Chapter 8, an insight piece plays a key role in the Wonder Leads process. To recap, its purpose is to back up the great opening impression made by the video with something of genuine substance. The insight piece achieves this by providing relevant, original and high-value content that educates the prospect and shows your expertise – essential in marking you out as a person of *real value*.

This chapter assumes that the insight piece has been created already. (If this isn't the case, you might choose to revisit Chapter 8, which guides the creation process. If it's still a work-in-progress but you want to keep pushing ahead, skip straight to Chapter 18; you can always return to this chapter once the insight is ready to share.)

If your insight piece is complete, the next section will guide you through working out the best way to introduce it.

Insight sharing message structure

You'll be sending your insight piece to every prospect who has been contacted, whether or not they previously responded, but this isn't an opportunity to follow up on the video – that ship has sailed. There is a chance that sharing your insight piece might encourage a small minority of prospects who hadn't previously seen your video to go back and check it out; but if they haven't felt the need to view it after receiving the original share message and nudge, they're highly unlikely to watch it now.

Nonetheless, a connection to the prospect exists that still has potential for a more meaningful relationship. Your insight piece should help to achieve just that.

An insight piece should offer something of genuine value, whether it helps the recipient solve a challenging problem, or look at their world through a different lens. In sharing this valuable resource for free, you're offering a gesture of support and friendship which hopefully will be acknowledged with a response – tiny conversational sparks light the way to more significant relationships.

There are very few downsides to sharing insight in this way. The main thing to be careful of is making the message look like yet another sales follow-up. Here's how to do it well.

1. OPENING

If you've already initiated a two-way conversation with the prospect, it's good practice to start with a positive observation. It could be something they're working on that was mentioned in a previous message, or something newsworthy published in their LinkedIn activity, such as awards, events or promotion campaigns – these are all great things to drop into a conversation. For example, "Hello Marc, congratulations on the new job – I hope it's started well." This kind of genuine attentiveness makes people feel valued, creating affirming, reciprocal feelings.

If your prospect hasn't replied to any messages yet, a simple, polite introduction is the order of the day, for example: "Hi Natalie, I hope you're well." Little touches can make all the difference in short messages, such as 'you're' instead of 'you are' – it's a tiny detail, but it helps make the statement less formal.

2. PURPOSE STATEMENT

The next task is to say why you're messaging – at this point, go ahead and introduce the insight piece. The exact wording will depend on the form that the insight piece takes: for example, if it's a white paper, your purpose statement might read: "I thought you might like a free copy of our new publication, 'Engineering Customers'."

Here, the language shows that we've created the publication; while saying it's free makes it clear that we're not expecting anything from the prospect in return.

3. VALUE STATEMENT

We've identified that every insight piece should offer intrinsic value to the reader, so we need to explain what that is. It might be advice on pending changes to current working methods, or highlighting how specific improvements can lead to significant cost savings, or offering them a previously unseen view of the competitive landscape. Whatever the benefit might be, it needs to be articulated in the most succinct way possible. For example, "It is a guide for businesses that want to improve B2B lead generation and attract more high-value prospects."

The important part is including a description to get the prospect's attention.

4. CLOSE

It takes considerable time and effort to create a good insight piece, but rest assured, it's time well spent. Of course, there is no guarantee that your contact will be interested in it, for various reasons: lack of time, existing knowledge, possibly even mistaking it for spam. Accepting this upfront means you can introduce the insight with understanding, for example: "I hope you find it useful." Being open-ended, this gives the recipient room to say whether it has helped or not, and makes it much easier for them to respond.

All that remains is an appropriately polite and professional ending. By this stage you'll have sent at least three previous messages to the prospect, so it's fine to keep it relatively informal: for example, 'Kind regards, Dave'.

The template below can help you get started – feel free to make it your own.

INSIGHT SHARING MESSAGE TEMPLATE

Hi [PROSPECT NAME],

I hope you're well.

I thought you might like a free copy of our new publication, [INSIGHT NAME].

It is a [VALUE STATEMENT].

I hope you find it useful.

Kind regards,

[YOUR NAME]

Timing an insight share

The advice for timing an insight sharing message is the same as sharing your nudge: leave it as long as possible (see Chapter 16, 'Timing your nudges'). While we're re-establishing contact with a prospect, sharing our insight piece is not a follow-up to earlier messages – with that in mind, traditional sales continuity is irrelevant. All that matters is breaking the mould of every standard approach that the prospect inevitably receives.

At the time of writing, I find myself the unfortunate target of a particularly relentless barrage of cold calling. At least three times a week, different people from the same company with whom I have never done business ring and ask to speak to me.

203

> I sigh, and joke with my reception team how horrific it must be to work for that company. It's pretty clear that all I am to them is means of fulfilling a quota – they will never get me as a customer, because life's too short to work with people who show so little respect.
>
> Sadly, this company is just one of many that set the tone.

A report published by sales and marketing research and advisory organisation, TOPO, seems to advocate 16 approaches to the same contact within a two to four-week period as the ideal formula for high-growth companies.[1] *Sixteen in less than 28 days.*

Put it this way: if you want others to hear your company name and shudder, be my guest. If you want to build a business that people look up to, find a better way: both your prospects and your self-respect deserve it.

Back to the insight piece: how long should you leave it? As a rule of thumb, at least three months after the last contact with the prospect. That's plenty of time for life to happen, wheels to turn and decisions to be made. It's also enough time for your presence to gently recede into the background, so that when contact is re-established, they might even be pleased to hear from you. Few salespeople can demonstrate genuine patience – the opportunity to break the mould is waiting for those that can.

> Just under a third of all prospects who viewed their video sent an additional response to the insight share. Some of these were from prospects who had not previously responded to either the initial sharing message or the nudge.
>
> It's clear that an insight piece offers a different level of value to the prospect and encourages a different type of response. It's also clear that we should never expect continuous engagement to every communication we send: a further signal that every one we do send *must* count!

ACTION POINTS

~~~

1. **Make the value clear.** Ensure your message clarifies why the insight piece you are sending will make their life better.
2. **Be generous with your knowledge.** The information you're sending is free and you don't require anything in return.
3. **Be precise.** Ensure all the details in your message are correct: check that you've attached or included the right link to your insight.
4. **Leave it as long as you can.** Three months is an ideal time from your previous communication, as this avoids being a pest.
5. **Use the Wonder Leads Insight Sharing Message Template** to structure the right message.

Now we've looked at what it takes to engage and cultivate more meaningful professional relationships through positive communication, all that's left is to enjoy the results.

To do that, we need to start *measuring*.

PART VII

MEASURING

207

18

Introduction to Measuring

t's time for a virtual fist bump, because you now know how to create an entire Wonder Leads campaign – including the best ways to connect, film, edit, publish and share information with prospects, and all the ingredients you need for generating incredible B2B leads.

There's just one final question to consider: how will we know if it's all been worth the effort?

Like all things that matter, Wonder Leads requires an investment of time – and as anyone in business knows, time is money. To get the most out of the process we need to know if that money was well spent: recording what is happening will tell us.

Spending time on activity that may not appear to yield direct benefits can feel like an imposition: measurement often falls into that category, especially in marketing circles. The problem is, without feedback from thorough measurement, all we're doing is shooting in the dark. We can't understand the in-depth trends and patterns that help us get the most out of every second invested in Wonder Leads. We can't learn from mistakes or benefit from successes either. Measuring is critical to get the best out of the Wonder Leads process.

Recording activity

Perfecting anything is as much about learning to fail as it is to succeed.

The inventor James Dyson released his first Dual Cyclone vacuum cleaner in 1993: it took 15 years and 5,126 failed attempts before finally creating one that worked. That would never have been possible if he hadn't recorded everything along the way: it gave him the ability to learn from trial and error.

Dyson didn't allow each failure to weigh him down; he simply viewed it as another step closer to a solution. That wouldn't have been possible by improvising every time: he probably would have thrown in the towel well before 100 iterations, let alone more than 5,000.

Consider Wonder Leads in the same way: by committing to this approach you're committing to your long-term success. It will take some extra time, but the rewards that come with knowing what *not* to do will repay you many times over.

If you're using YouTube, Vimeo or landing pages hosted on your website (see Chapter 14), the best tool for recording activity is a spreadsheet. (To accompany this book, a free Wonder Leads Activity Log is available to get you started: see the Resources section for download details.)

Let's look at how to keep track.

1. CONNECTIONS

Here, 'connection' means the prospects you are specifically targeting, rather than contacts made along the way – so only log the prospects who have *accepted* a connection request, rather than *sent* requests. Not everyone will accept a request, so registering everyone before they do wastes time and complicates data management unnecessarily.

Log your prospects by order of connection date: this makes it easier to manage your communication schedule because the right people will be next to each other in the spreadsheet. This way, updating data for an entire batch of approaches is much quicker: they're already in logical order, so no need to jump around a dataset.

Depending on how deep you want to go into the analysis, you could also log the *day* of the connection acceptance. This can be useful for understanding prospects' contact preferences and planning your schedule more effectively.

> The majority of my connection requests are accepted on a Tuesday (28 per cent), closely followed by Monday (24 per cent), then Wednesday (20 per cent). By far the lowest weekday is Friday: I only receive 5 per cent of connection acceptances on that day.
>
> As I'm generally looking to contact people within a week of connecting, usually I aim to send out introductions on a Monday or Tuesday. The above statistics tell me that my targets are most engaged on LinkedIn at the start of the week: not only is this data I can leverage for my Wonder Leads, but all my other LinkedIn marketing activity too.

2. SCRIPTS

Do keep track of the scripts used for each introduction. Over time, they will inevitably adapt and evolve – perhaps due to new statistics for a case study, or by experimenting with new introduction and closing statements. Depending on your business, you might need different scripts for different market sectors or products. Keeping track of script variations enables you to identify the ones that generate the most responses and leads: they can be used more frequently, making the whole process more effective.

While making a note of the script you're using, also mark whether you have *personalised* your script to that individual. This helps you to see the enormous difference that personalisation can make to overall performance (see Chapter 9, 'Personalise whenever you can').

> Because I know which videos I have (and haven't) personal-
> ised, every minute I've invested in personalising a video has
> been worth it: they deliver better response rates, lead-genera-
> tion rates and three times the number of positive comments.

3. SHARING

Keep a log of your sharing activity, starting with the date of your
initial share, as it allows you to schedule your nudges. For example, if
you send the initial message on 1 January and are working to a four-
week gap for nudges, this tells you the exact date when those nudges
need to go out. Similarly, once you have sent a nudge, you know when
to schedule sharing your insight piece.

This is key: if you don't log when communications are going
out, the entire process could descend into chaos.

4. VIEWS (REACH)

In Wonder Leads, tracking your landing page views helps to work
out the all-important reach rate. Reach is a metric that refers to the
number of people exposed, at least once, to a medium during a given
period. Reach is a factor in any outbound lead-generation campaign,
but it often appears in a different guise. For example, in online advertising it's referred to as 'impressions', in event advertising, 'footfall',
and in email marketing, 'opens'. In cold calling circles, it's best recognised as 'connections'.

Reach is a flawed metric

The problem with reach as a metric is that its significance varies,
depending on the medium in question. That makes it quite easy to
manipulate. In Chapter 1 we examined the problem with traditional
methods of business development: it's worth recapping some of these
points here to understand why Wonder Leads is much more precise.

For example, email opens are a pretty good indication that the message reached the intended recipient. Of course, tracking email opening is not foolproof, so there's likely to be a significant margin of error – but in general, email is a reasonably direct one-to-one approach. An event might have a footfall of 10,000 people, but unless every delegate meets the target profile and passes by a business's stand, reach will be a fraction of that. In theory, every time someone answers a cold call, they have been reached – but in reality, the prospect is only reached when that caller manages to speak to the intended person. (If you've ever tried cold calling, you'll know only too well that this is a tiny percentage most of the time.)

These anomalies crop up all the time whenever reach is studied. It's so easy to be seduced by this metric, because it can fool us into thinking that we're speaking to a lot more prospects than we actually are.

> *In B2B lead generation, the only thing that matters is talking to the right people. Everything else is just noise.*

Use reach rate instead

Instead of comparing reach in terms of isolated numbers, the only real way to formulate a judgement of each tactic is to analyse reach *rate*: the number of views against the size of the audience being contacted, expressed as a percentage. For example, if you send a communication to 1,000 people and 300 of them view it, the reach rate is 30 per cent. Comparing reach rates for different lead-generation tactics is far more helpful, because it indicates how effective they are at converting effort into results.

Table 2 compares reach rates for the most commonly used, proactive business development tactics: it shows that Wonder Leads is nearly three times more effective at reaching the right people than the next best alternative. This may sound suspiciously high, but it's really not.

Table 2: Comparison of reach rate statistics for different proactive lead-generation activities[1]

	Cold calling	E-marketing	Direct mail	Wonder Leads
Reach rate	**6%**	**21%**	–	**55%**

The beauty of Wonder Leads is that the sender knows they are speaking to the right people because they've been hand-picked. They know which prospects have been *reached* because each prospect has a unique landing page. All the sender needs to do is record when that landing page receives a visit, and chalk one up in the 'reach' column for that approach.

Tracking views

There are a few ways to monitor views, depending on how the landing pages are published. With Vimeo or YouTube, it should be possible to check the impressions for videos through the 'user statistics' panel. Do bear in mind that as a sender, your views of a video page may be included in those numbers, so personal visits need to be discounted from the results.

For those using landing pages on a company website, it should be a simple case of checking the analytics. Again, be mindful of polluting the data with internal visits; if you're using a platform such as Google Analytics, you can exclude internal traffic from appearing in reports.[2] This means being able to test and visit live landing pages without mistaking your views for those of your prospect.

With Socialaser, all views are tracked instantly through the system. The 'view rate' (as reach rate is referred to in Socialaser) is visible from the main dashboard and updated automatically every time a new view is recorded. Notifications are sent whenever a first live view is recorded, which means you don't have to waste time manually tracking visitor activity. The software also comes with a preview function, which means never having to worry about internal visits to landing pages corrupting data.

It's very possible that some prospects' landing pages will be viewed multiple times – this doesn't affect reach rate. As Wonder Leads is a bespoke approach, reach is a binary option: either the prospect sees a landing page, or they don't. Still, it can be useful to record repeat visits, as they can indicate that a prospect is particularly fond of the approach, or might have shared it with colleagues. This also helps to identify those prospects that warrant even closer attention.

5. RESPONSES

In Wonder Leads, a response is any form of reply to a sharing message. It can be the simplest of acknowledgements, such as a "Thanks" or thumbs-up emoji, or a longer reply with a "Thanks, but no thanks" sentiment. It doesn't matter so long as there is one, because a two-way conversation has been initiated.

This can be leveraged, unlike many other lead-generation efforts that fail to start any sort of dialogue. Generally, how many replies do you see to marketing emails or direct mail campaigns that say, "Thanks, but I'm not interested"? Almost none. No one is compelled to reply, because the amount of personal consideration that goes into creating and sending a typical outbound campaign simply doesn't warrant it.

215

Table 3: Comparison of response rate statistics for different proactive lead-generation activities[3]

	Cold calling	E-marketing	Direct mail	Wonder Leads
Response rate	**6%**	**2.6%**	**3%**	**44%**

Table 3 compares the response rate statistics for outbound business development techniques against my results using Wonder Leads. It shows that Wonder Leads is:

- 7 times more effective than cold calling
- 14 times more effective than direct mail
- More than 16 times more effective than e-marketing

Unlike the other methods, which are notoriously difficult to record responses accurately, Wonder Leads responses are easy to measure, being direct replies from the personal account of a target prospect.

Responses are the lifeblood of any lead-generation campaign, so recording every single one is vital. Every reply is a sign that stronger relationships are being built with the people that matter. Over time, it's impossible to overestimate the positive impact that such relationships have on a business.

Segmenting responses

Rather than lumping all responses into one, it's a good idea to segment them: it helps you see the points at which prospects tend to reply, which makes it easier to hone your approach. The four segments to consider are as follows.

First-time responses

It's useful to know who your first-time responders are, because they tend to be the most active LinkedIn users, and the ideal people on whom to concentrate your relationship-building efforts.

> Currently, 38 per cent of all my viewed videos receive a first-time response. These are received on average within 3.7 days of sharing the video.

Nudge responses

Monitoring your nudges helps you to see if they're performing as effectively as they should be.

> 33 per cent of all my viewed videos receive a response after I have sent a nudge. On average, it takes just 2.2 days to receive those responses after delivering the nudge.
>
> This highlights why nudging is so important. It also shows that prospects feel compelled to respond more quickly – most likely because they don't wish to appear rude by ignoring a second friendly message.

Insight piece responses

Being able to see which people have responded to your insight sharing messages helps you assess the impact of your insight piece. If the response numbers are low, it's possible your insight piece might need further work to offer greater value.

> It took me an average of just 1.1 days to receive a reply to an insight piece share, which indicates that high-value content may compel people to respond sooner, most likely driven by the Law of Reciprocity.

Positive responses

Noting the responses that include particular praise for the approach is helpful, as they're a clear sign that you've made a strong impression on the prospect. Of course, while this doesn't *guarantee* a sales opportunity, it does at least indicate a stronger connection which can be developed even further over time.

> Examples of affirming replies I've received from prospects include the following:
>
> > "Hi Dave, I just wanted to tell you that I thought that was an excellent introduction video, and you differentiated yourself very well from others that approach me!"
>
> and
>
> > "Dave, that is the best intro approach *ever* through LinkedIn."
>
> In total, 33 per cent of all approaches where I can confirm that a prospect has viewed their video generated a positive response. This means that one-third of Wonder Leads receiving a view result in forming a powerful connection with the prospect.
>
> No other form of business development I've encountered can even quantify that, let alone compete with it.

6. LEADS

There is little more exciting in the sales and marketing world than recording a genuine sales opportunity. In the Wonder Leads process, it's vital to record every lead to understand the generation rate: being across this data helps you comprehend how many introductions to make on average to generate a genuine sales opportunity; it also supports you in judging your business development efforts. As mentioned previously, you want to know that everything you're doing is worth the effort.

Unfortunately, lead-generation rates for traditional forms of business development are usually meagre and often impossible to quantify.

Table 4: Comparison of lead generation statistics for different proactive lead-generation activities[4]

	Cold calling	E-marketing	Direct mail	Wonder Leads
Lead generation rate	**0.6%**	–	–	**10.8%**

Table 4 compares lead-generation rates for traditional business development activities versus Wonder Leads. As mentioned previously, the limit of measurement data available for email marketing and direct mail on a B2B sale level is response rate: there are no reliable statistics to explain how many of those responses turn into leads. All that we can say is that the number of leads generated will be a percentage of those figures. In other words, a slice of 2.6 per cent for email marketing, and a slice of 3 per cent for direct mail. My educated guess is that lead generation rates for these methods will be less than 1%: if they were significantly higher than cold calling, nobody would bother making cold calls – but sadly we know that they do, every day.

The absence of data for e-marketing and direct mail leaves us with cold calling as the only reliable comparison to Wonder Leads. As the table shows, Wonder Leads is 18 times more effective at generating leads than cold calling. We know this is accurate, because sales opportunities arrive straight into the LinkedIn inbox. This not only proves that quality will always trump quantity, but it is possible to achieve incredible business development results without resorting to activities that many people find objectionable. Not all of the leads generated through Wonder Leads have been immediate sales opportunities, but they clearly indicate that prospects welcome further discussion. For example:

> "Loved the personal message, Dave – very
> impressed – I don't think we are at the right time
> at the moment, but would be interested to meet up
> when back in the UK late May."
> "Hi Dave, would love to have a call and see if there
> is any synergy in terms of our objectives. I'm tied
> up until Friday but happy to chat then?"
>
> For the type of work that I do, these kinds of responses are
> the only type of lead I could expect. No one gets their cheque-
> book out straightaway.

7. THE FINER DETAILS

The concept of 'marginal gains' is often attributed to Sir Dave Brails-
ford, currently general manager of the professional cycling outfit,
Team INEOS, and former director of British Cycling. His '1% Philosophy'[5] explains how focusing on the seemingly smaller details can
make a massive difference to overall results. Whatever our opinion of
such an approach (and elite cycling has had more than its fair share
of skeletons in the closet), there is no denying the benefits.

The same kind of philosophy applies to analysing Wonder
Leads. It involves taking a bit of extra time to monitor the seemingly trivial factors which, cumulatively, make a significant difference
to performance. Here are some of the metrics within that bracket.

———

Appearance

Do you ever look in the mirror in the morning and wonder if what
you're wearing is going to make the right impression at the big meeting that day? As we discussed in Chapter 11, it almost certainly will.

What we choose to wear has far-reaching psychological impli-
cations, so it makes sense to keep a log of what you've worn during
filming: this means you can examine which combination of clothes
leads to the best results.

I tested nine different outfit combinations while filming my videos. I achieved the highest percentage of responses while wearing a dark green shirt without a jacket or sweater: 53 per cent of all the videos received a reply.

The same dark green shirt coupled with a navy jacket was the next best, followed by a navy polo shirt with a navy sweater. The lowest percentage of responses was when I wore a pink T-shirt and a blue jacket. (Clearly, not all men can pull off pink!)

Time

To keep track of efficiency, it makes sense to monitor time by running the occasional time-in-motion study.

It took me the best part of a day to film my first five introductions, plus another day to edit and create the landing pages; a week later, I had recorded 15 videos in less than an hour, and published and shared them all within 2 hours. The improvement curve was pretty steep.

A few weeks into the process, I wanted to see how long everything was taking, so I recorded the time it took to complete each of the processes during an entire batch of videos. I covered everything from finding a prospect to inputting the results.

This data was eye-opening. It took me on average 16 minutes 9 seconds to create and manage one introduction. The longest parts of the process were filming and making connections. The next most time-consuming tasks were editing videos, uploading and processing, creating landing pages and monitoring and updating analytics.

This data not only helps with planning, but makes it possible to work out how long it takes to generate a response and a lead.

Using my current response rate of 44 per cent means that I should get a response for every 37 minutes I spend on the Wonder Leads process. My current lead-generation rate of 10.8 per cent means that I'm generating a lead for every 2 hours 29 minutes I spend. All I have to do is work out how many leads I want each month, and plan my schedule accordingly.

Time-in-motion data was the primary driver behind the creation of Socialaser: to make the process faster and much more efficient.

Equipment

As we saw in Chapter 10, filming requires a lot of equipment. While you might not think it necessary, making a note of what you're using can be useful in case different combinations generate more responses than others. For example, you might choose to compare different mics or lighting set-ups.

Admittedly, this is niche analysis, but any improvement could end up paying big dividends down the line by making every approach more effective.

Location

For those with access to multiple filming locations, it might be useful to keep a record of where each video is recorded. This identifies those backdrops eliciting the best responses, so you can concentrate on filming there more regularly.

Domains

Socialaser gives access to multiple domain names to host landing pages, so you can test the impact of different ones to see which get the best response rates.

For example, you can see the difference it makes using your company domain name, compared with a personalised one such as my 'from-dave.to'. You can even compare it to one of the in-built domains available through Socialaser, such as 'from-me.to', 'myvideo.to' or 'myintro.to'. (For up-to-date analysis on the comparative effectiveness of different domains, please check out the Wonder Leads blog.)[††]

ACTION POINTS

~~~~

1. **Organise from the start.** The more prepared you are, the easier and faster the process is to manage, and the more introductions you'll be able to send.
2. **Learn from the findings.** Build on all the things that work, no matter how small. Take advantage of the 'marginal gains' philosophy to improve effectiveness, as every improvement means generating leads more efficiently.
3. **Use the Wonder Leads Activity Log** to help you record all of your activity if using YouTube, Vimeo or your own website.
4. **Consider using a system like Socialaser** to cut administration time, automate tasks, access deeper personalisation levels and hit the ground running.

EPILOGUE

I never had any ambitions to become an author. When I started my Wonder Leads journey, my only motivation was generating quality new leads for my business. When I began to get responses, it quickly became apparent that I had stumbled across something far more significant than me and my small business.

I know full well that I'm not the only business owner who has struggled with business development: there are plenty, even in my tiny corner of the world. Multiply that across the globe, and there must be hundreds of thousands, if not millions of people, just like me. Businesspeople looking to showcase their abilities proactively, in a way that doesn't alienate the very people they are trying to attract.

Wonder Leads is an incredibly powerful framework. All I ask is that you use it the way I intended: to help raise the bar. For too long, B2B sales has become reliant on a quick-win mentality, chasing empty promises of incredible rewards for minimal effort. *Nothing* that matters comes easy. Yes, you can improve things with knowledge and the right tools but ultimately, great rewards only come with great application.

This system will not work for you if all you are interested in is cutting corners. If you don't spend the time to craft messages, learn scripts or personalise videos, it will fail. If you bombard your prospect with follow-ups of no value, or don't spend time to record activity, it will fail.

The precise reason that Wonder Leads is so effective is that it *does* require your time. The difference is that unlike almost any other type of business development, you know it's time well spent.

I wish you good luck on your new path to success, and whatever you do – always be positive.

NOTES

Introduction

1.　Benjamin Snyder (2017) '7 insights from legendary investor Warren Buffett', CNBC, 1 May. Available at: www.cnbc.com/2017/05/01/7-insights-from-legendary-investor-warren-buffett.html

Chapter 1

1.　Gordon Tredgold (2017) '20 lessons learned from making 2,000 B2B cold calls in just 20 days', Entrepreneur, 21 June. Available at: www.entrepreneur.com/article/295992

2.　Mailchimp's email marketing benchmark report compares performance across a full spectrum of industries and business sizes. By analysing the performance of hundreds of millions of emails sent via its system each month, Mailchimp can provide accurate performance statistics for email marketing campaigns. Mailchimp (2020) 'Email marketing benchmarks by industry'. February. Available at: https://mailchimp.com/resources/email-marketing-benchmarks

3.　Debora Haskel (2017) 'Know your customers or you're "just talking," says the 2017 DMA Response Report', IWCO Direct, 25 July. Available at: www.iwco.com/blog/2017/07/25/2017-dma-response-rate-report/

4.　Bizzabo (2019) 'The 2019 Event Marketing Report: Benchmarks and trends'. Available at: https://welcome.bizzabo.com/event-marketing-2019

5.　Center for Exhibition Industry Research (CEIR) (2018) '2018 Marketing Spend Decision Report'. Available at: https://store.ceir.org/marketing-spend-decision-report-2018

6.　Display Wizard (2020) '20 amazing trade show statistics that will blow your mind!'. Available at: www.displaywizard.co.uk/20-amazing-trade-show-statistics

7.　Colin Matthes (2018) '20 powerful stats on the value of trade shows and expos', SpinGo, 2 March. Available at: www.spingo.com/blog/post/20-powerful-stats-on-the-value-of-trade-shows-and-expos

8.　Center for Exhibition Industry Research (CEIR) data, in iCapture (2020) 'Trade shows matter', 21 January. Available at: www.icapture.com/resources/articles/trade-shows-matter

9.　FaceTime (nd) 'The power of live events', infographic. Available at: www.facetime.org.uk/__media/Research/FaceTime_POWER-OF-EVENTS-Guide.pdf

10.　Trade Shows News Network (2012) 'CEIR's latest report indicates attendees prefer face-to-face interaction with exhibitors', 19 September. Available at: https://www.tsnn.com/news/ceirs-latest-report-indicates-attendees-prefer-facetoface-interaction-exhibitors

11.　Laura Ramos with Peter O'Neill, Matthew Camuso and Peggy Dostie (2016) '2016 B2B budget plans show that it's time for a digital wake-up call', Forrester, 21 July. Available at: www.forrester.com/report/2016+B2B+Budget+Plans+Show+That+Its+Time+For+A+Digital+WakeUp+Call/-/E-RES119354#

12.　Display Wizard, '20 amazing trade show statistics that will blow your mind!'

13. BNI UK (2020) 'BNI: The world's leading business networking and referral organisation'. Available at: https://bni.co.uk/en-GB/index

14. In Great Business Schools (2020) 'Face squared – The numbers behind face to face networking', infographic. Available at: https://greatbusinessschools.org/networking/

15. Derek Coburn (2016) 'Why networking events are a waste of time, and what to do instead', the *Guardian*, 17 November. Available at: www.theguardian.com/small-business-network/2016/nov/17/why-networking-events-are-a-waste-of-time-and-what-to-do-instead

16. Zenith Media (2019) 'Advertising expenditure forecasts March 2019'. Available at: www.zenithmedia.com/wp-content/uploads/2019/03/Adspend-forecasts-March-2019-executive-summary.pdf

17. Zenith Media, 'Advertising expenditure forecasts March 2019'.

18. Caroline Cakebread (2019) 'B2Bs aren't spending big on digital advertising (yet)', eMarketer, 30 January. Available at: www.emarketer.com/content/b2bs-aren-t-spending-big-on-digital-advertising-yet

19. Business Information Network (BIN) report data, Connectiv. Available at: www.siia.net/Divisions/Connectiv-Business-Information-Association-of-SIIA/BIN-Reports

20. Mimi An (2016b) 'Why people block ads (and what it means for marketers and advertisers)', HubSpot. Available at: https://blog.hubspot.com/marketing/why-people-block-ads-and-what-it-means-for-marketers-and-advertisers

21. Dan Shewan (2017) 'The comprehensive guide to online advertising costs', WordStream, 20 April. Available at: www.wordstream.com/blog/ws/2017/07/05/online-advertising-costs

22. Kristen Herhold (2018) "How businesses use online advertising in 2018', The Manifest, 14 August. Available at: https://themanifest.com/digital-marketing/how-businesses-use-online-advertising

23. Digital Marketing Institute (2017) 'Digital leaders share their insights on digital transformation success'. Available at: https://digitalmarketinginstitute.com/blog/digital-leaders-share-their-insights-on-digital-transformation-success

24. Julia Manoukian (2017) 'The ROI of social selling: 5 data-driven outcomes [infographic]', Sales for Life, 7 September. Available at: www.salesforlife.com/blog/the-roi-of-social-selling-5-data-driven-outcomes-in-2017-infographic

25. Aria Solar (2019) 'Infographic: Social selling statistics to validate & strengthen your strategy', Sprout Social. Available at: https://sproutsocial.com/insights/social-selling-statistics

Chapter 2

1. BrightTALK (2015) 'B2B lead generation: Trends report'. Available at: http://go.brighttalk.com/rs/105-RTY-982/images/Holger_B2B_Lead_Gen_Report.pdf

2. HubSpot (2018) 'State of inbound marketing', report. Available at: www.stateofinbound.com/

3. Mike Michalowicz (2018) Clockwork: Design Your Business to Run Itself, Portfolio.

4. Megan Golden (2016) 'The case for B2B marketing on LinkedIn [infographic]', LinkedIn, 16 November. Available at: https://business.linkedin.com/marketing-solutions/blog/linkedin-b2b-marketing/2016/

get-proof--the-case-for-b2b-marketing-on-linkedin--infographic-

5.   LinkedIn (2017) 'The sophisticated marketer's guide to LinkedIn'. Available at: https://business.linkedin.com/content/dam/me/business/en-us/marketing-solutions/cx/2017/pdfs/Sophisticated-Marketers-Guide-to-LinkedIn-v03.12.pdf

6.   Content Marketing Institute (2018) '2018 Benchmarks, Budgets and Trends – North America'. Available at: https://contentmarketinginstitute.com/wp-content/uploads/2017/09/2018_B2B_Research_FINAL.pdf

7.   HubSpot (2012) 'State of inbound marketing' report. Available at: www.hubspot.com/state-of-marketing

8.   Oktopost, in HipB2B (2014) 'LinkedIn for B2B Lead Generation – Why, When, How?', infographic. Available at: www.hipb2b.com/blog/infographic-linkedin-b2b-lead-generation

Chapter 3

1.   Wonder Leads (2020) 'How Wonder Leads crushes traditional B2B business development'. Available at: https://wonderleads.com/comparison

2.   Dave Holloway (2019) 'Engineering customers: How manufacturers can influence the B2B buying process to attract more high-value prospects', BML Creative. Available at: https://bml-creative.co.uk/engineering-customers-b2b-lead-generation-guide/

Chapter 5

1.   J. O'Doherty, J. Winston, H. Critchley, D. Perrett, D.M. Burt and R.J. Dolan (2003) 'Beauty in a smile: The role of medial orbitofrontal cortex in facial attractiveness'. *Neuropsychologia* 41(2): 147–155.

2.   Marianne Sonnby-Borgström (2008) 'Automatic mimicry reactions as related to differences in emotional empathy'. *Scandinavian Journal of Psychology* 43(5): 433–443.

Chapter 6

1.   Nicholas Toman, Brent Adamson and Cristina Gomez (2017) 'The new sales imperative', *Harvard Business Review*, March–April. Available at: https://hbr.org/2017/03/the-new-sales-imperative

Chapter 7

1.   Tim Askew (2017) 'The magic of manners', Inc.com. Available at: www.inc.com/tim-askew/the-magic-of-manners.html

2.   Mario Martinez Jr (2016) 'How I get a 74% acceptance on new connection requests', Vengreso.com, 21 May. Available at: https://vengreso.com/blog/get-74-acceptance-new-connection-requests

3.   Ingrid Lunden (2017) 'LinkedIn hits 500M member milestone for its social network for the working world', Tech Crunch, 24 April. Available at: https://techcrunch.com/2017/04/24/linkedin-hits-500m-member-milestone-for-its-social-network-for-the-working-world/

Chapter 8

1. Robert McKee (2020) 'Is it possible to bring storytelling into marketing?' Available at: https://mckeestory.com/is-it-possible-to-bring-storytelling-into-marketing/

2. Seth Godin, in Larry Kim (2020) '50 inspirational business quotes from Gates, Winfrey, Musk, and More', Inc.com. Available at: www.inc.com/larry-kim/50-inspirational-business-quotes-from-gates-winfrey-musk-amp-more.html

3. Dave Holloway (2019) 'Engineering customers: How manufacturers can influence the B2B buying process to attract more high-value prospects', BML Creative. Available at: https://bml-creative.co.uk/engineering-customers-b2b-lead-generation-guide/

4. Matthew Dixon and Brent Adamson (2013) *The Challenger Sale: How to Take Control of the Customer Conversation*, Portfolio.

5. Matthew Dixon, Brent Adamson, Pat Spenner and Nick Toman (2015) *The Challenger Customer: Selling to the Hidden Influencer Who Can Multiply Your Results*, Penguin.

Chapter 9

1. Dale Carnegie (2006[1936]) *How to Win Friends and Influence People*, Vermilion.

2. Dennis P. Carmody and Michael Lewis (2006) 'Brain activation when hearing one's own and others' names'. *Brain Research* 1116(1): 153–158. Available at: www.sciencedirect.com/science/article/abs/pii/S0006899306022682?via%3Dihub

3. Simon Sinek (2011) *Start with Why: How Great Leaders Inspire Everyone to Take Action*, Penguin.

4. Microsoft (2015) 'Attention spans: Consumer insights, Microsoft Canada', spring. Available at: http://dl.motamem.org/microsoft-attention-spans-research-report.pdf

5. Mimi An (2016a) 'Buyers speak out: How sales needs to evolve', HubSpot. Available at: https://blog.hubspot.com/sales/buyers-speak-out-how-sales-needs-to-evolve

6. Arthur I. Gates (1917) 'Recitation as a factor in memorizing', Columbia University.

7. Jeffrey Vocell (2018) 'Personalized calls to action perform 202% better than basic CTAs [New Data]', HubSpot. Available at: https://blog.hubspot.com/marketing/personalized-calls-to-action-convert-better-data

8. Andrew Davies (2013) 'Three major benefits of using personalisation in marketing', Econsultancy, 12 August. Available at: https://econsultancy.com/three-major-benefits-of-using-personalisation-in-marketing/

9. Seth Godin (2014) '...different people differently'. Seth's Blog, 27 January. Available at: https://seths.blog/2014/01/different-people-differently/

10. Brian Tracy (2020) 'Using the law of reciprocity and other persuasion techniques correctly'. Available at: https://www.briantracy.com/blog/sales-success/using-the-law-of-reciprocity-and-other-persuasion-techniques-correctly/

Chapter 10

1. Steve Peters (2012) *The Chimp Paradox: The Acclaimed Mind Management Programme to Help You Achieve Success, Confidence and Happiness*, Vermilion.

2. The Wandering Albatross (*Diomedea exulans*) has the largest wingspan of any bird at 3.65 metres.

3.   Justin Simon (2017) 'How to get the perfect lighting for video', TechSmith. Available at: www.techsmith.com/blog/get-perfect-lighting-video/

Chapter 11

1.   David A. Frederick, Gaganjyot Sandhu, Patrick J. Morse and Viren Swami (2016) 'Correlates of appearance and weight satisfaction in a U.S. national sample: Personality, attachment style, television viewing, self-esteem, and life satisfaction'. *Body Image* 17(June): 191–203. Available at: www.sciencedirect.com/science/article/abs/pii/S1740144516301498

2.   M.W. Kraus and W.B. Mendes (2014) 'Sartorial symbols of social class elicit class-consistent behavioral and physiological responses: A dyadic approach'. *Journal of Experimental Psychology: General* 143(6): 2330–2340. Available at: https://psycnet.apa.org/record/2014-38364-001

Chapter 12

1.   Alison Wood Brooks (2014) 'Get excited: Reappraising pre-performance anxiety as excitement'. *Journal of Experimental Psychology: General* 143(3): 1144–1158. Available at: www.apa.org/pubs/journals/releases/xge-a0035325.pdf

2.   Jacqueline Whitmore (2013) 'Sound advice: How to make your voice more effective', Entrepreneur, 27 September. Available at: www.entrepreneur.com/article/228515

3.   Kim Lachance Shandrow (2019) '7 powerful public speaking tips from one of the most-watched TED Talks speakers', Entrepreneur, 6 March. Available at: www.entrepreneur.com/slideshow/299610

4.   Whitmore, 'Sound advice: How to make your voice more effective'.

5.   Lachance Shandrow, '7 powerful public speaking tips from one of the most-watched TED Talks speakers'.

6.   Joe Navarro (2012) *The Power of Body Language: An Ex-FBI Agent's System for Speed-reading People*, Simon & Schuster/Nightingale-Conant.

7.   Caroline Goyder (2014) *Gravitas: Communicate with Confidence, Influence and Authority*, Vermilion.

8.   Toastmasters International (2011) 'Gestures: Your body speaks – how to become skilled in nonverbal communication'. Available at: www.toastmasters.org/-/media/files/department-documents/education-documents/201-gestures.ashx

9.   Toastmasters International, (2011) 'Gestures: Your body speaks'. – how to become skilled in nonverbal communication'. Available at: www.toastmasters.org/-/media/files/department-documents/education-documents/201-gestures.ashx

10.   Jared Matthew Weiss, in Brandon Smith (2013) 'Top 10 tips for being awesome on camera', Mashable, 27 July. Available at: https://mashable.com/2013/07/27/camera-tips/

Chapter 13

1.   Microsoft (2018) 'Remove sound from a video'. Available at: https://answers.microsoft.com/en-us/windows/forum/all/remove-sound-from-a-video/6eeff8ac-acdf-47ab-8d7e-2259b4074fc7

Chapter 14

1. LinkedIn Marketing Solutions (nd) 'Your audience is on LinkedIn'. Available at: https://business.linkedin.com/marketing-solutions/audience

2. Abraham Maslow (1943) 'A theory of human motivation'. *Psychological Review* 50(4): 370–396.

3. Bitly (2020) 'Increasing engagement: The power of custom domains'. Available at: https://bitly.com/pages/resources/casestudies/ increasing-engagement-the-power-of-a-branded-short-domain

Chapter 15

1. Rudolph A. Pyatt Jr (1990) 'Companies finding that failure to communicate with investors can be costly', *Washington Post*, 15 November. Available at: www. washingtonpost.com/archive/business/1990/11/15/companies-finding-that-failure-to-communicate-with-investors-can-be-costly/0b458fa3-76db-45c6-a817-557dcdba1f4c/

2. Scott M. Cutlip and Allen H. Center (1952) *Effective Public Relations: Pathways to Public Favor*, Prentice-Hall.

3. Forbes Insights (2010) 'Video in the C Suite: Executives embrace the non-text web'. Available at: https://i.forbesimg.com/forbesinsights/StudyPDFs/Video_in_the_ CSuite.pdf

4. LinkedIn Official Blog (2020) 'New Features To Make Your LinkedIn Messaging Experience Even Better'. Available at https://blog.linkedin.com/2020/september/24/ new-features-to-make-your-linkedin-messaging-experience-even-better

Chapter 16

1. Mimi An (2016a) 'Buyers speak out: How sales needs to evolve', HubSpot. Available at: https://blog.hubspot.com/sales/buyers-speak-out-how-sales-needs-to-evolve?_ ga=2.158616191.458722835.1579689480-2088008605.1578326058

2. Irene Scopelliti, George Loewenstein and Joachim Vosgerau (2015) 'You call it "self-exuberance"; I call it "bragging": Miscalibrated predictions of emotional responses to self-promotion'. *Psychological Science*, 7 May. Available at: https://journals.sagepub. com/doi/abs/10.1177/0956797615573516

3. Steli Efti (2020) 'Master the sales follow-up with this proven formula (Tells you exactly when and how to follow up for maximum results)', Close.com. Available at: https://blog.close.com/follow-up

Chapter 17

1. TOPO (2016) 'The 2016 sales benchmark development report'. Available at: https:// hosteddocs.emediausa.com/Sales-Development-Benchmark-Report-Sponsored-By-Outreach.pdf

Chapter 18

1. Gordon Tredgold (2017) '20 lessons learned from making 2,000 B2B cold calls in just 20 days', Entrepreneur Europe, 21 June. Available at: https://www.entrepreneur.com/article/295992 • Mailchimp (2020) 'Email marketing benchmarks by industry', February. Available at: https://mailchimp.com/resources/email-marketing-benchmarks/ • Debora Haskel (2017) 'Know your customers or you're "just talking," says the 2017 DMA Response Report', IWCO Direct, 25 July. Available at: www.iwco.com/blog/2017/07/25/2017-dma-response-rate-report/

2. Google Analytics (nd) 'Exclude internal traffic: Filter out traffic to your website from people on your corporate network'. Available at: https://support.google.com/analytics/answer/1034840?hl=en

3. Tredgold, '20 lessons learned from making 2,000 B2B cold calls in just 20 days'. • Mailchimp, 'Email marketing benchmarks by industry'. • Haskel, 'Know your customers or you're "just talking"'.

4. Tredgold, '20 lessons learned from making 2,000 B2B cold calls in just 20 days'. • Mailchimp, 'Email marketing benchmarks by industry'. • Haskel, 'Know your customers or you're "just talking"'.

5. Matt Slater (2012) 'Olympics cycling: Marginal gains underpin Team GB dominance', BBC Sport, 8 August. Available at: www.bbc.co.uk/sport/olympics/19174302

BIBLIOGRAPHY

An, Mimi (2016a) 'Buyers speak out: How sales needs to evolve', HubSpot. Available at: https://blog.hubspot.com/sales/buyers-speak-out-how-sales-needs-to-evolve

An, Mimi (2016b) 'Why people block ads (and what it means for marketers and advertisers)', HubSpot. Available at: https://blog.hubspot.com/marketing/why-people-block-ads-and-what-it-means-for-marketers-and-advertisers

Askew, Tim (2017) 'The magic of manners', Inc.com. Available at: www.inc.com/tim-askew/the-magic-of-manners.html

Bitly (2020) 'Increasing engagement: The power of custom domains'. Available at: https://bitly.com/pages/resources/casestudies/increasing-engagement-the-power-of-a-branded-short-domain

Bizzabo (2019) 'The 2019 Event Marketing Report: Benchmarks and trends'. Available at: https://welcome.bizzabo.com/event-marketing-2019

BNI UK (2020) 'BNI: The world's leading business networking and referral organisation'. Available at: https://bni.co.uk/en-GB/index

BrightTALK (2015) 'B2B lead generation: Trends report'. Available at: http://go.brighttalk.com/rs/105-RTY-982/images/Holger_B2B_Lead_Gen_Report.pdf

Business Information Network (BIN) report data, Connectiv. Available at: www.siia.net/Divisions/Connectiv-Business-Information-Association-of-SIIA/BIN-Reports

Cakebread, Caroline (2019) 'B2Bs aren't spending big on digital advertising (yet)', eMarketer, 30 January. Available at: www.emarketer.com/content/b2bs-aren-t-spending-big-on-digital-advertising-yet

Carmody, Dennis P. and Lewis, Michael (2006) 'Brain activation when hearing one's own and others' names'. *Brain Research* 1116(1): 153–158. Available at: www.sciencedirect.com/science/article/abs/pii/S0006899306022682?via%3Dihub

Carnegie, Dale (2006[1936]) *How to Win Friends and Influence People*, Vermilion.

Center for Exhibition Industry Research (CEIR) (2018) '2018 Marketing Spend Decision Report'. Available at: https://store.ceir.org/marketing-spend-decision-report-2018

Coburn, Derek (2014) *Networking Is Not Working: Stop Collecting Business Cards and Start Making Meaningful Connections*, Idea Press.

Coburn, Derek (2016) 'Why networking events are a waste of time, and what to do instead', the *Guardian*, 17 November. Available at: www.theguardian.com/small-business-network/2016/nov/17/why-networking-events-are-a-waste-of-time-and-what-to-do-instead

Content Marketing Institute (2018) '2018 Benchmarks, Budgets and Trends – North America'. Available at: https://contentmarketinginstitute.com/wp-content/uploads/2017/09/2018_B2B_Research_FINAL.pdf

Cutlip, Scott M. and Center, Allen H. (1952) *Effective Public Relations: Pathways to Public Favor*, Prentice-Hall.

Davies, Andrew (2013) 'Three major benefits of using personalisation in marketing', Econsultancy, 12 August. Available at: https://econsultancy.com/three-major-benefits-of-using-personalisation-in-marketing/

Digital Marketing Institute (2017) 'Digital leaders share their insights on digital transformation success'. Available at: https://digitalmarketinginstitute.com/blog/digital-leaders-share-their-insights-on-digital-transformation-success

Display Wizard (2020) '20 amazing trade show statistics that will blow your mind!'. Available at: www.displaywizard.co.uk/20-amazing-trade-show-statistics

Dixon, Matthew and Adamson, Brent (2013) *The Challenger Sale: How to Take Control of the Customer Conversation*, Portfolio.

Dixon, Matthew, Adamson, Brent, Spenner, Pat and Toman, Nick (2015) *The Challenger Customer: Selling to the Hidden Influencer Who Can Multiply Your Results*, Penguin.

Efti, Steli (2020) 'Master the sales follow-up with this proven formula (Tells you exactly when and how to follow-up for maximum results', Close.com. Available at: https://blog.close.com/follow-up

FaceTime (nd) 'The power of live events', infographic. Available at: www.facetime.org.uk/__media/Research/FaceTime_POWER-OF-EVENTS-Guide.pdf

Forbes Insights (2009) 'Business meetings: The case for face-to-face'. Available at: https://i.forbesimg.com/forbesinsights/StudyPDFs/Business_Meetings_FaceToFace.pdf

Forbes Insights (2010) 'Video in the C Suite: Executives embrace the non-text web'. Available at: https://i.forbesimg.com/forbesinsights/StudyPDFs/Video_in_the_CSuite.pdf

Frederick, David A., Sandhu, Gaganjyot, Morse, Patrick J. and Swami, Viren (2016) 'Correlates of appearance and weight satisfaction in a U.S. national sample: Personality, attachment style, television viewing, self-esteem, and life satisfaction'. *Body Image* 17(June): 191–203. Available at: www.sciencedirect.com/science/article/abs/pii/S1740144516301498

Gates, Arthur I. (1917) 'Recitation as a factor in memorizing', Columbia University.

Godin, Seth (2014) '...different people differently'. Seth's Blog, 27 January. Available at: https://seths.blog/2014/01/different-people-differently/

Godin, Seth, in Kim, Larry (2020) '50 inspirational business quotes from Gates, Winfrey, Musk, and More', Inc.com. Available at: www.inc.com/larry-kim/50-inspirational-business-quotes-from-gates-winfrey-musk-amp-more.html

Golden, Megan (2016) 'The case for B2B marketing on LinkedIn [infographic]', LinkedIn, 16 November. Available at: https://business.linkedin.com/marketing-solutions/blog/linkedin-b2b-marketing/2016/get-proof--the-case-for-b2b-marketing-on-linkedin--infographic-

Google Analytics (nd) 'Exclude internal traffic: Filter out traffic to your website from people on your corporate network'. Available at: https://support.google.com/analytics/answer/1034840?hl=en

Goyder, Caroline (2014) *Gravitas: Communicate with Confidence, Influence and Authority*, Vermilion.

Haskel, Debora (2017) 'Know your customers or you're "just talking," says the 2017 DMA Response Report', IWCO Direct, 25 July. Available at: www.iwco.com/blog/2017/07/25/2017-dma-response-rate-report/

Herhold, Kristen (2018) ''How businesses use online advertising in 2018', The Manifest, 14 August. Available at: https://themanifest.com/digital-marketing/how-businesses-use-online-advertising

Holloway, Dave (2019) 'Engineering customers: How manufacturers can influence the B2B buying process to attract more high-value prospects', BML Creative. Available at: https://bml-creative.co.uk/engineering-customers-b2b-lead-generation-guide/

HubSpot (2012) 'State of inbound marketing' report. Available at: www.hubspot.com/state-of-marketing

HubSpot (2018) 'State of inbound marketing', report. Available at: www.stateofinbound.com/

Kraus, M.W. and Mendes, W.B. (2014) 'Sartorial symbols of social class elicit class-consistent behavioral and physiological responses: A dyadic approach'. *Journal of Experimental Psychology: General* 143(6): 2330–2340. Available at: https://psycnet.apa.org/record/2014-38364-001

Lachance Shandrow, Kim (2019) '7 powerful public speaking tips from one of the most-watched TED Talks speakers', Entrepreneur, 6 March. Available at: www.entrepreneur.com/slideshow/299610

LinkedIn (2017) 'The sophisticated marketer's guide to LinkedIn'. Available at: https://business.linkedin.com/content/dam/me/business/en-us/marketing-solutions/cx/2017/pdfs/Sophisticated-Marketers-Guide-to-LinkedIn-v03.12.pdf

LinkedIn Marketing Solutions (nd) 'Your audience is on LinkedIn'. Available at: https://business.linkedin.com/marketing-solutions/audience

Lunden, Ingrid (2017) 'LinkedIn hits 500M member milestone for its social network for the working world', Tech Crunch, 24 April. Available at: https://techcrunch.com/2017/04/24/linkedin-hits-500m-member-milestone-for-its-social-network-for-the-working-world/

Mailchimp (2020) 'Email marketing benchmarks by industry', February. Available at: https://mailchimp.com/resources/email-marketing-benchmarks/

Manoukian, Julia (2017) 'The ROI of social selling: 5 data-driven outcomes [infographic]', Sales for Life, 7 September. Available at: www.salesforlife.com/blog/the-roi-of-social-selling-5-data-driven-outcomes-in-2017-infographic

Martinez Jr, Mario (2016) 'How I get a 74% acceptance on new connection requests', Vengreso.com, 21 May. Available at: https://vengreso.com/blog/get-74-acceptance-new-connection-requests

Maslow, Abraham (1943) 'A theory of human motivation'. *Psychological Review* 50(4): 370–396.

Matthes, Colin (2018) '20 powerful stats on the value of trade shows and expos', SpinGo, 2 March. Available at; www.spingo.com/blog/post/20-powerful-stats-on-the-value-of-trade-shows-and-expos

McKee, Robert (2020) 'Is it possible to bring storytelling into marketing?' Available at: https://mckeestory.com/is-it-possible-to-bring-storytelling-into-marketing/

Michalowicz, Mike (2018) *Clockwork: Design Your Business to Run Itself*, Portfolio.

Microsoft (2015) 'Attention spans: Consumer insights, Microsoft Canada', spring. Available at: http://dl.motamem.org/microsoft-attention-spans-research-report.pdf

Microsoft (2018) 'Remove sound from a video'. Available at: https://answers.microsoft.com/en-us/windows/forum/all/remove-sound-from-a-video/6eeff8ac-acdf-47ab-8d7e-2259b4074fc7

Navarro, Joe (2012) *The Power of Body Language: An Ex-FBI Agent's System for Speed-reading People*, Simon & Schuster/Nightingale-Conant.

O'Doherty, J., Winston, J., Critchley, H., Perrett, D., Burt, D.M. and Dolan, R.J. (2003) 'Beauty in a smile: The role of medial orbitofrontal cortex in facial attractiveness'. *Neuropsychologia* 41(2): 147–155.

Oktopost, in HipB2B (2014) 'LinkedIn for B2B Lead Generation – Why, When, How?', infographic. Available at: www.hipb2b.com/blog/infographic-linkedin-b2b-lead-generationPeters, Steve (2012) *The Chimp Paradox: The Acclaimed Mind Management Programme to Help You Achieve Success, Confidence and Happiness*, Vermilion, p. 48.

Pyatt Jr., Rudolph A. (1990) 'Companies finding that failure to communicate with investors can be costly', *Washington Post*, 15 November. Available at: www.washingtonpost.com/archive/business/1990/11/15/companies-finding-that-failure-to-communicate-with-investors-can-be-costly/0b458fa3-76db-45c6-a817-557dcdba1f4c/

Ramos, Laura with O'Neill, Peter, Camuso, Matthew and Dostie, Peggy (2016) '2016 B2B budget plans show that it's time for a digital wake-up call', Forrester, 21 July. Available at: www.forrester.com/report/2016+B2B+Budget+Plans+Show+That+Its+Time+For+A+Digital+WakeUp+Call/-/E-RES119354#

Scopelliti, Irene, Loewenstein, George and Vosgerau, Joachim (2015) 'You call it "self-exuberance"; I call it "bragging": Miscalibrated predictions of emotional responses to self-promotion'. *Psychological Science*, 7 May. Available at: https://journals.sagepub.com/doi/abs/10.1177/0956797615573516

Shewan, Dan (2017) 'The comprehensive guide to online advertising costs', WordStream, 20 April. Available at: www.wordstream.com/blog/ws/2017/07/05/online-advertising-costs

Simon, Justin (2017) 'How to get the perfect lighting for video', TechSmith. Available at: www.techsmith.com/blog/get-perfect-lighting-video/

Sinek, Simon (2011) *Start With Why: How Great Leaders Inspire Everyone to Take Action*, Penguin.

Slater, Matt (2012) 'Olympics cycling: Marginal gains underpin Team GB dominance', BBC Sport, 8 August. Available at: www.bbc.co.uk/sport/olympics/19174302

Smith, Brandon (2013) 'Top 10 tips for being awesome on camera', Mashable, 27 July. Available at: https://mashable.com/2013/07/27/camera-tips/

Snyder, Benjamin (2017) '7 insights from legendary investor Warren Buffett', CNBC, 1 May. Available at: www.cnbc.com/2017/05/01/7-insights-from-legendary-investor-warren-buffett.html

Solar, Aria (2019) 'Infographic: Social selling statistics to validate & strengthen your strategy', Sprout Social. Available at: https://sproutsocial.com/insights/social-selling-statistics

Sonnby-Borgström, Marianne (2008) 'Automatic mimicry reactions as related to differences in emotional empathy'. *Scandinavian Journal of Psychology* 43(5): 433–443.

Toastmasters International (2011) 'Gestures: Your body speaks – how to become skilled in nonverbal communication'. Available at: www.toastmasters.org/-/media/files/department-documents/education-documents/201-gestures.ashx

Toman, Nicholas, Adamson, Brent and Gomez, Cristina (2017) 'The new sales imperative', *Harvard Business Review*, March–April. Available at: https://hbr.org/2017/03/the-new-sales-imperative

TOPO (2016) 'The 2016 sales benchmark development report'. Available at: https://hosteddocs.emediausa.com/Sales-Development-Benchmark-Report-Sponsored-By-Outreach.pdf

Tracy, Brian (2020) 'Using the law of reciprocity and other persuasion techniques correctly'. Available at: https://www.briantracy.com/blog/sales-success/using-the-law-of-reciprocity-and-other-persuasion-techniques-correctly/

Trade Shows News Network (2012) 'CEIR's latest report indicates attendees prefer face-to-face interaction with exhibitors', 19 September. Available at: https://www.tsnn.com/news/ceirs-latest-report-indicates-attendees-prefer-facetoface-interaction-exhibitors

Tredgold, Gordon (2017) '20 lessons learned from making 2,000 B2B cold calls in just 20 days', Entrepreneur, 21 June. Available at: www.entrepreneur.com/article/295992

Vocell, Jeffrey (2018) 'Personalized calls to action perform 202% better than basic CTAs [New Data]', HubSpot. Available at: https://blog.hubspot.com/marketing/personalized-calls-to-action-convert-better-data

Whitmore, Jacqueline (2013) 'Sound advice: How to make your voice more effective', Entrepreneur, 27 September. Available at: www.entrepreneur.com/article/228515

Wonder Leads (2020) 'How Wonder Leads crushes traditional B2B business development'. Available at: https://wonderleads.com/comparison

Wood Brooks, Alison (2014) 'Get excited: Reappraising pre-performance anxiety as excitement'. *Journal of Experimental Psychology: General* 143(3): 1144–1158. Available at: www.apa.org/pubs/journals/releases/xge-a0035325.pdf

Zenith Media (2019) 'Advertising expenditure forecasts March 2019'. Available at: www.zenithmedia.com/wp-content/uploads/2019/03/Adspend-forecasts-March-2019-executive-summary.pdf

RESOURCES

A series of free, downloadable resources accompany this book to help you through the various stages of the Wonder Leads process. It includes all the tools referenced throughout in a handy online pack to print out and scribble on to your heart's content.

To access yours, visit: wonderleads.com/freestuff

I've also set up a LinkedIn group for people who are implementing, or considering implementing, the Wonder Leads framework for their business. It serves as a forum to share ideas, best practice and personal experiences, so that everyone can enjoy the benefits of positive communication. Just request an invitation via: linkedin.com/groups/8868252

Finally, if you have any thoughts, comments or experiences to share about Wonder Leads, I would love to hear from you – especially if you have stories of how it may have helped you.

Website: wonderleads.com

Twitter: twitter.com/wonderleads

Facebook: facebook.com/wonderleads

LinkedIn: linkedin.com/company/wonderleads

ACKNOWLEDGEMENTS

There would be no Wonder Leads without my amazing wife, Natalie. Not only has she been my soulmate for nearly 20 years, but my business partner for three-quarters of that time. We've been through some tremendous ups and downs, both personally and professionally. How she has put up with me through it all truly defies imagination. She is intelligent, warm and funny, with a selfless caring for others that's rarely to be found.

Of course, she's far too modest to say any of these things herself, so that's why I'm telling you. Ever since we got together, I've known that I've been punching well above my weight. All I can do is thank her for believing in me, and helping me to be the best version of myself that I can. This book is really down to her.

I would also like to pay special thanks to my editor, Lisa Cordaro. Writing a book for the first time and handing it over to someone else for scrutiny is a daunting prospect. From the very first communication we had, Lisa was able to grasp the vision I had for the project. Her encouragement, professionalism and sharp business acumen have helped to make this book far better than it otherwise would have been.

Huge thanks must also go to Quinn Daley from Fish Percolator for their outstanding work developing our Socialaser software. Quinn is one of those rare individuals; whose intelligence and ability is matched only by their kindness of spirit. The world needs more people who are capable of changing it for the better. Quinn is unquestionably one.

Over the past few years I've engaged in a huge amount of self-education. The work of Simon Sinek, Andy Cope, Rob Moore, Emma Gannon, Paul Jarvis, Michael Port and Marty Neumeir (to name but a few) have all provided eye-opening revelations which have helped to inspire the writing of this book. In particular, I'd like to single out Seth Godin, whose writing has been instrumental in reshaping my perspective of marketing and business in general.

To all those like him, who are generous enough to share their knowledge with the world – I offer my unwaivering gratitude.

ABOUT THE AUTHOR

Dave Holloway is a graduate of the University of Wolverhampton, where he achieved a First Class Honours degree in Graphic Communication. Since 2007, together with his wife, Natalie, Dave has run the award-winning brand communications agency, BML Creative. He has worked with global B2B companies including Linde plc, Kantar Group and Croda International plc, as well as leading institutions such as the NHS, The Royal British Legion and the University of London. His expertise in brand strategy and design has helped numerous businesses to grow exponentially.

Dave is a firm believer in social responsibility, and helped to set up Prints for Charity (printsforcharity.shop) – a website which has raised thousands of pounds for local charities through the sale of artwork created by the BML team.

He lives in Yorkshire with Natalie and their two children.

INDEX

Socialaser®

Start incredible conversations

MORE WONDER LEADS IN LESS TIME

Socialaser® makes the creation, management, delivery and measurement of Wonder Leads faster, simpler and even more effective.

Everything you need to start opening incredible sales conversations:

PERSONALISED EVERYTHING	**POWERFUL REPORTING**	**RAPID MESSAGING**	**VIDEO HOSTING**
Create and launch live landing pages in seconds. Access customised scripts, messages and domains from a single interface.	Instantly see your View, Response, Click and Lead-Generation rates. See which introductions, scripts and messages perform best.	Create template sharing messages. Autofill, copy, paste and reach out directly to prospects at the touch of a button.	No more switching between software platforms. Upload, store and host your Wonder Leads videos alongside your landing pages.

TRY IT FOR FREE!
Visit: wonderleads.com/socialaser

Printed in Great Britain
by Amazon

60272599R00149